Narzu Tarannum
Nova Ahmed

Efficient and Reliable Cloud Architecture for Big Data Handling

Narzu Tarannum
Nova Ahmed

Efficient and Reliable Cloud Architecture for Big Data Handling

Framework, Implementation

LAP LAMBERT Academic Publishing

Impressum / Imprint

Bibliografische Information der Deutschen Nationalbibliothek: Die Deutsche Nationalbibliothek verzeichnet diese Publikation in der Deutschen Nationalbibliografie; detaillierte bibliografische Daten sind im Internet über http://dnb.d-nb.de abrufbar.

Bibliographic information published by the Deutsche Nationalbibliothek: The Deutsche Nationalbibliothek lists this publication in the Deutsche Nationalbibliografie; detailed bibliographic data are available in the Internet at http://dnb.d-nb.de.

Coverbild / Cover image: www.ingimage.com

Verlag / Publisher:
LAP LAMBERT Academic Publishing
ist ein Imprint der / is a trademark of
OmniScriptum GmbH & Co. KG
Bahnhofstraße 28, 66111 Saarbrücken, Deutschland / Germany
Email: info@lap-publishing.com

Herstellung: siehe letzte Seite /
Printed at: see last page
ISBN: 978-3-659-81703-8

Zugl. / Approved by: Dhaka, North South University, Bangladesh, 2013

Contents

Overview

The objective of this book is to implement and experiment a hybrid Cloud computing framework which is feasible and necessary to handle huge data. A prototype system using national ID database structure of Bangladesh which is prepared by Election Commission (EC) of Bangladesh is discussed. Hybrid cloud architecture is presented and justified with adequate feasibility analysis and each of the modules of the prototype system is implemented and experimented in different chapters. The infrastructure of newly presented hybrid cloud divides into two parts: locally hosted cloud and remote cloud. Remote cloud would discuss with the experiment with Elastic MapReduce (EMR) of Amazon Web Service (AWS). Eucalyptus infrastructure would discuss for local cloud. Both of these structures of cloud computing is handled by apache Hadoop. Hadoop is presented with both EMR and HortonWorks Data Platform (HDP) where database is implemented by HiveQL. User information visibility, authorization and authentication issues are considered for the prototype system for searching people of Bangladesh in different purpose. So, considering EC's database the prototype application named Bangladesh People Search (BDPS) is managed by a hybrid structure of cloud computing handled by apache hadoop. The complete implementation of such a system is presented step by step.

Chapter-1

1. Introduction

Cloud computing is an emerging concept for Computer network arena. Data distribution, authentication and authorization [2] are major challenges to implement an application based on public database. We proposed an Efficient and Reliable Hybrid Cloud Architecture for big Database [1]. In this work we considered national ID database, prepared by election commission (EC) of Bangladesh [22]. We implemented different modules of the system and experimented with a prototype in this book. We also discuss some experimental findings to justify our previous proposal [22]. The structure of our proposed architecture divided into two parts. One infrastructure is locally implemented using open source "Eucalyptus" [11], [17] and the other part of the infrastructure will be implemented on Amazon Web Service (AWS) [14] cloud. In a country like Bangladesh power failure and as well as internet connection failure are common problem. Data traffic congestion, SQL server time out issue and as a result server down is very frequent for any kind of national level searching issue like Higher Secondary school Certificate, TIN registration issue etc.

National level information access through database is an international challenge. This happened because of the risk of single server failure. To defend these problems we proposed the Hybrid cloud Structure for BDPS which will be handled by apache Hadoop [13], [15], [21]. Apache Hadoop is an open-source software framework that supports data-intensive distributed applications. It supports the running of applications on large clusters of commodity hardware. The Hadoop framework transparently provides both reliability and data motion to applications. Hadoop implements a computational paradigm named map-reduce [13], where the application is divided into many small fragments of work, each of which may be executed or re-executed on any node in the cluster. In addition, it provides a distributed file system that stores data on the compute nodes, providing very high aggregate bandwidth across the cluster. Both map-reduce and the distributed file systems are designed so that node failures are automatically handled by the framework. It enables applications to work with thousands of computation-independent computers and petabytes of data. To address the [4] authentication and authorization issue and make EC's Database in more effective, efficient and useful, we consider following ideas: 1. Everyone will have a password to access their information and take a printout in a specific format to

7

use in official purpose. 2. Everyone can only check others information by entering info. 3. Academic, Job information, Criminal record can be entered and verified by same database. Figure 1.1 is showing the hybrid infrastructure for handling big data.

We considered national ID database for searching Bangladeshi People in different purpose. An interactive web based application prototype by using hybrid structure of cloud computing has implemented in our research which is based on Hadoop with Elastic MapReduce (EMR). We used four elastic (EC2) nodes or instances that are installed on Amazon Web Service (AWS). All the nodes including the head node is installed on CentOS verstion-6.3 operating system for HortonWorks data platform to implement local cloud part. To address the authentication we also enabled public key and private key tool.

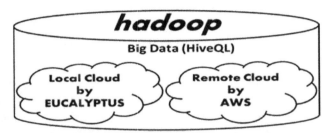

Figure 1.1: Hybrid Structure of Cloud for Handling Big Data

In our research we proposed a hybrid structure of cloud computing as depicted in figure-1.2. This structure is divided into two parts. One infra-structure will be locally implemented by using "Eucalyptus" and the other part of the infra-structure will be implemented in well-known Amazon Web Service (AWS) cloud. On top of this infra-structure Hadoop framework would be used to implement the system. In our structure the solid lined servers are representing the "always on" server. In local elastic cloud part those servers will be used for query handling requested by the users and in External AWS cloud those server will be used for backup and mirroring. In local elastic cloud part dashed line servers will be used as elastic computer which will be automatically "UP" as needs' basis. The number of server will depend on the number of query request. In External AWS cloud the dashed server will be used is case of overflow request and in case of local cloud infra-structure failure. Any kind of Linux server can be used for this implementation. We used Debian Linux in our prototype cloud and Hadoop implementation. HiveQL is the preferable database for our proposed system but we used MySQL for our prototype. Different type of devices around Local Elastic Cloud indicates that our system would support entire computing platform.

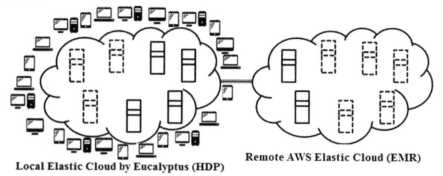

Local Elastic Cloud by Eucalyptus (HDP)   **Remote AWS Elastic Cloud (EMR)**

Figure 1.2 : Hybrid architecture of cloud

One important issue in our application was the visibility. Since it is general software and everyone have access to this database, visibility of other's information became an important issue. A unique solution is proposed and implemented to address this issue in our research as follow:

Following steps are followed to implement the BDPS Application:

1. Register with AWS.

2. Install EC2 instances on AWS.

3. Operating System and Network configuration using Putty.

4. a. Install Hadoop with HortonWorks Data Platform (HDP) in four CenOS instances.

b. Lunch Amazon Elastic MapReduce service in Debian Large machine.

5. Develop the application in a single Windows-2008 Server instance.

6. Deploy the system on the cloud.

7. Experiment and Result Analysis.

1.1. Basic Concept

1.1.1. What is Cloud Computing?

Cloud computing is a universal term for anything that demands delivering hosted services over the Internet. Cloud computing provide resources and service on an as needs' basis. It is an Internet based computing environment where you pay only for resources that you use. Resource allocation can be adjusted.

The cloud computing model is one of the very important shapes of a new era. This technology based on the distributed computing, parallel computing and grid computing.

The revolutionary prospect of cloud computing is changing the way of people's thought in IT. Day by day, the amount of data stored at companies like Google, Yahoo, Facebook, Amazon or Twitter has become incredibly huge. The new challenging requirement of this 'Big Data' era make us realize to rethink what we require of a database, and to come up with answers aside from the relational databases that have served us well for a quarter of century. Thus, web applications and databases in cloud are undergoing major architectural changes to take advantage of the scalability provided by the cloud.

1.1.2. Benefits of Cloud Computing

Cloud computing platforms possess characteristics of both clusters and Grids, with its own special attributes and capabilities such strong support for virtualization, dynamically compo sable services with Web Service interfaces, and strong support for creating 3rd party, value added services by building on Cloud compute, storage, and application services. Thus, Clouds are promising to provide services to users without reference to the infrastructure on which these are hosted.

Overall, Cloud Computing can lead to reduced costs and access to resources that perhaps any company would have difficulty in funding or finding difficult to justify.

1.1.3. Goal

As a class project, we developed a web base application called people search for Bangladesh using very few partial data based on National ID. We included some unique features in that application for authorization. After getting some experience we realized that the system should be stable, secured and scalable. In 2013 government declared that every income tax payee should have an online TIN number which information will be verified from our National ID Database. We found that in rush hour system crashed and a number of people could not get their online TIN in due time. We also observed that in recent years government is declaring the result of national examinations like SSC, HSC, BSc under National University through web-site and SMS which was a very positive initiative for our society. But again the same problem was happening in rush hour the service became unavailable or having a huge delay. Those situations have given us the motivation of using Elastic computing. We found Cloud Computing is the solution for it but due the lack of resources and support it was very complicated for us to implement cloud. Suddenly we got a guideline to use Amazon Web Service. We registered with them and were able to use their free services. Again we found that the free services are not sufficient enough implement our system and it would be very expensive for our research. Than we got education grant from AWS in different steps and got our final motivation to reach our goal.

1.1.4. Deployment model for BDPS

BDPS will make the database available to the general people by using the public cloud. Here Election Commission or a National Data Center will be the service provider. These services are free for General people to access their information. Election Commission or a National Data Center can introduce a fee for new registration and update process. Since a number of agencies will use this database, a huge amount of revenue is also possible. BDPS will also offer a pay-per-use model for the corporate user who will use this database frequently for information verification. Considering scenario we proposed a hybrid cloud structure as a deployment model for our System.

BDPS own and operate the infrastructure and offer access only via Internet. 3G internetwork is available in almost everywhere. So, very expensive infrastructure is not necessary for this system.

1.1.5. Service Model for BDPS: (Issue of SaaS, PaaS, IaaS)

Cloud computing providers offer their services according to three fundamental models. Since PaaS helped to run the application on the web and also provide application development toolkits, we choose PaaS as a service model for BDPS. The user of BDPS does not manage or control the underlying cloud infrastructure including network, servers, operating systems, or storage, but has control over the deployed applications.

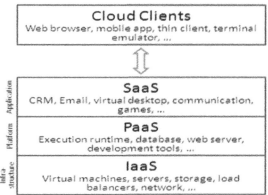

Figure 1.3: Service Model

1.2. Outline:

This book is formatted in following way: - chapter 2 discusses about motivation and literature review, chapter 3 describes the Implementation Preparation, we proposed architecture in chapter 4 and Implementation on AWS; Install Hadoop with HortonWorks Data Platform (HDP), the experiment of Hadoop on MapReduce is discussed in chapter 5, chapter 6 describes about our implemented prototype system and chapter 7 discusses about evaluation. In this book appendix-I contains the GUIs, HTML and PHP code for our prototype system. Output report for HiveQL will be found in appendix-II. NeatBeans installation steps are shown in appendix-III.

Chapter-2

2. Motivation

Cloud computing [12] is a universal term for anything that demands delivering hosted services over the Internet. Cloud computing provide resources and service on an as needs' basis. It is an Internet based computing environment where we pay only for resources that we use. Resource allocation can be adjusted. Day by day, the amount of data stored at companies like Google, Yahoo, Facebook, Amazon or Twitter has become incredibly huge. The new challenging requirement of this 'Big Data' era make us realize to rethink what we require of a database, and to come up with answers aside from the relational databases that have served us well for a quarter of century. Thus, web applications and databases in cloud are undergoing major architectural changes to take advantage of the scalability provided by the cloud.

Cloud computing platforms possess characteristics of both clusters and Grids, with its own special attributes and capabilities such strong support for virtualization, dynamically compo sable services with Web Service interfaces, and strong support for creating 3rd party, value added services by building on Cloud compute, storage, and application services. Thus, Clouds are promising to provide services to users without reference to the infrastructure on which these are hosted. Overall, Cloud Computing can lead to reduced costs and access to resources that perhaps any company would have difficulty in funding or finding difficult to justify. Considering those features we proposed architecture and justified the feasibilities in our previous work [1]. We considered AWS and Windows Azure for Remote cloud implementation. Amazon Web Services (AWS) [14] is a collection of remote computing services that together make up a cloud computing platform, offered over the Internet by Amazon.com. AWS is located in 8 geographical 'Regions'. Availability Zones are isolated from each other to prevent outages from spreading between Zones. Windows Azure [16] is a cloud computing platform and infrastructure, created by Microsoft, for building, deploying and managing applications and services through a global network of Microsoft-managed datacenters.

Open Source has advantages like leverage the work of a growing community of developers, works across multiple hardware infrastructures, possible to deploy at service providers and on-premise, customized to fit individual needs or to add additional services etc. So we considered Eucalyptus and Openstack for our model.

Eucalyptus [17] is open source software for building Amazon Web Services (AWS)-compatible private and hybrid clouds. It allows an organization to build self-service, elastic clouds inside its datacenter using existing IT infrastructure. Openstack [18] is a collection of open source components to deliver public and private IaaS clouds whose components are Nova, Swift, Glance, Keystone, and Quantum. IaaS Cloud Services allows users to manage VMs, Virtual networks, storage resources etc.

From the above discussion we found that AWS and Windows Azure are the options to implement Remote cloud. Unfortunately the service of Windows Azure is not available in Bangladesh and the services are not only expensive but also limited comparing to AWS for our application. AWS made a number of resources available to the researchers some of them we used for our experiment which includes EC2, S3 etc. Different types of instances are verified for our application.

For local cloud, a comparative study by [26] Sonali Yadav is considered where the characteristics and performance is observed for Eucalyptus, Openstank and Opennebula. From that study we found that Eucalyptus would be better option for our proposed architecture because Eucalyptus provides an EC2 -compatible cloud Computing Platform and S3-compatible Cloud Storage thus its services are available through EC2/S3 compatible APIs. Eucalyptus can leverage (drag) a heterogeneous collection of virtualization technologies within a single cloud, to incorporate resources that have already been virtualized without modifying their configuration.

2.1. Research Background

2.1.1. Case Study1

Makhija et al. [4] discussed their methods of data security and privacy including different existing cloud components and methods. According to their review, they found many limitations on security mechanisms, lack in supporting dynamic data operations, data integrity. Considering all these limitations they proposed methods for ensuring data authentication using Third Party Auditor (TPA). Third Party Auditor is kind of inspector. TPA audits the data of client. Our proposed system would consider TPA for ensuring security and privacy issue. A message authentication codes (MACs) algorithm discussed by Mohta et al. [5] can be used to protect the data integrity and dynamic data operations. Provable data possession (PDP) method by Wang et al. [6] would be considered to ensure possession of data files on untrusted storages. Public key based homomorphic authenticator by Cong Wang et al. [7] and a schema "Proof of retrievability" for large files using "sentinels" proposed by Juels et al. [8] also considered for confirming the authentication and authorization issue in our system.In this research paper, they presented introduction to a cloud computing that is expected to be adopted by governments, manufacturers and academicians in the very near future. It directly affects the company, government and convenience to the small user.

It is the technology of building a robust data security between CSP(Cloud Service Provider) and User. This promising technology is literally called Cloud Data Security.

In this research, an introduction to the technology of Cloud Computing, TPA(Third Party Auditor), data security and security algorithm of different papers is presented.

2.1.1.1. Types of Service Model

Cloud computing providers offer their services according to three fundamental models Infrastructure as a service (IaaS), Platform as a service (PaaS) and software as a service SaaS) where IaaS is the most basic and each higher model abstracts from the details of the lower models.

1) Software as a Service (SaaS): The capability provided to the consumer is to use the provider's applications running on a cloud infrastructure. The applications are accessible from various client devices through either a thin client interface, such as a web browser, or a program interface.

2) Platform as a Service (PaaS): The capability provided to the consumer is to deploy onto the cloud infrastructure consumer-created or acquired applications created using programming languages, libraries, services, and tools supported by the provider. The consumer does not manage or control the underlying cloud infrastructure including network, servers, operating systems, or storage, but has control over the deployed applications and possibly configuration settings for the application-hosting environment.

3) Infrastructure as a Service (IaaS): The capability provided to the consumer is to provision processing, storage, networks, and other fundamental computing resources where the consumer is able to deploy and run arbitrary software, which can include operating systems and applications. The consumer does not manage or control the underlying cloud infrastructure but has control over operating systems, storage, and deployed applications; and possibly limited control of select networking components.

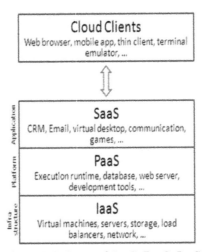

Figure 2.1: Issue of SaaS, PaaS, IaaS

2.1.1.2. Deployment Models in Cloud Computing:

Deployment models describe who owns, manages and is responsible for the services.

1) Private cloud: The cloud infrastructure is provisioned for exclusive use by a single organization comprising multiple consumers (e.g. business units). It may be owned, managed, and operated by the organization, a third party, or some combination of them, and it may exist on or off premises.

2) Public cloud: The cloud infrastructure is provisioned for open use by the general public. It may be owned, managed, and operated by a business, academic, or government organization, or some combination of them. It exists on the premises of the cloud provider.

3) .Community cloud: The cloud infrastructure is provisioned for exclusive use by a specific community of consumers from organizations that have shared concerns (e.g., mission, security requirements, policy, and compliance considerations). It may be owned, managed, and operated by one or more of the organizations in the community, a third party, or some combination of them, and it may exist on or off premises.

4) Hybrid cloud: Hybrid cloud infrastructure is a composition of two or more distinct cloud infrastructures (private, community, or public) that will be unique entities, but bound together by standardized technology that enables data and application portability (e.g., cloud bursting for load balancing between clouds)

16

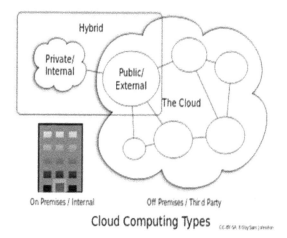

Cloud Computing Types

Figure 2.2: Issue of Private, Public, Hybrid Cloud

2.1.1.3. Third Party Auditor:

Data stored and retrieved may not be fully trustworthy so here concept of TPA (Third Party Auditor) is used. TPA makes task of client easy by verifying integrity of data stored on behalf of client.

Third Party Auditor is kind of inspector. TPA will audit the data of client.

It eliminates the involvement of the client by auditing that whether his data stored in the cloud are indeed intact, which can be important in achieving economies of scale for Cloud Computing. The released audit report would help owners to evaluate the risk of their subscribed cloud data services, and it will also be beneficial to the cloud service provider to improve their cloud based service platform .

TPA will help data owner to make sure that his data are safe in the cloud and management of data will be easy and less burdening to data owner.

2.1.1.4. Security Algorithms:

They discuss a simple approach like message authentication codes (MACs) can be used to protect the data integrity.

They discuss about the author Abhishek Mohta and R. Sahu who have given algorithm which ensures data integrity and dynamic data operations.

The author Ateniese et al are the first who have considered the public adaptability in their defined provable data possession(PDP) method which ensures possession of data files on untrusted storages.

The author Cong Wang et al. used the public key based homomorphic authenticator and to achieve a privacy-preserving public auditing system for cloud data storage security .

The author Ari Juels and Burton S. Kaliski Jr proposed a scheme "Proof of retrievability" for large files using "sentinels".

Conclusion: They explained different existing paper techniques and their merits and demerits. They discussed their methods of data security and privacy etc. In all those papers some haven't described proper data security mechanisms, some were lack in supporting dynamic data operations, some were lack in ensuring data integrity, while some were lacking by high resource and computation cost. Hence this paper gives overall clue of all existing techniques for cloud data security and methods proposed for ensuring data authentication using TPA.

2.1.2. Case Study2:

We studied and reviewed some articles before designing and developing our system. Buyyaa et al. [3] have proposed architecture for market-oriented allocation. Distributed of resources within Clouds are also discussed in their literature. They discussed on meta-negotiation infrastructure for global Cloud exchanges which can provide high performance content delivery via Storage Clouds. Various Cloud efforts to reveal its emerging potential for the creation of third-party services is also discussed. The architecture, service model are based on this discussion.

In Information and Communications Technology (ICT), there is an increasingly perceived vision that computing will one day be the 5th utility (after water, electricity, gas, and telephony). This computing utility, like all other four existing utilities, will provide the basic level of computing service that is considered essential to meet the everyday needs of the general community.

To deliver this vision, a number of computing paradigms have been proposed, of which the latest one is known as Cloud computing.

2.1.2.1. Contribution of this paper:

They have proposed architecture for market-oriented allocation of resources within Clouds.

They have also presented a vision for the creation of global Cloud exchange for trading services.

They have discussed some representative platforms for Cloud computing covering the state-of-the-art.

They have presented various Cloud efforts to reveal its emerging potential for the creation of third-party services.

18

They have presented meta-negotiation infrastructure for global Cloud exchanges and provide high performance content delivery via `Storage Clouds'.

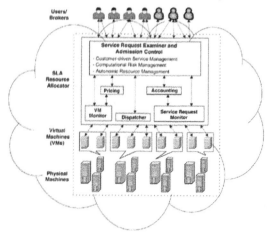

Figure 2.3: High-level market-oriented Cloud architecture

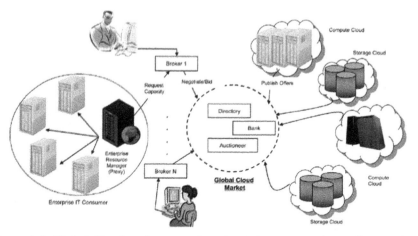

Figure 2.4: Global Cloud exchange and market infrastructure for trading services

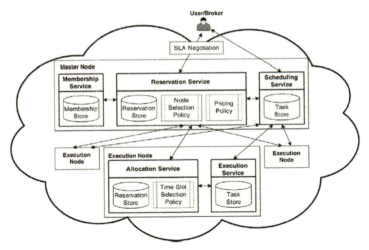

Figure 2.5: Interaction of services in Aneka Cloud environment.

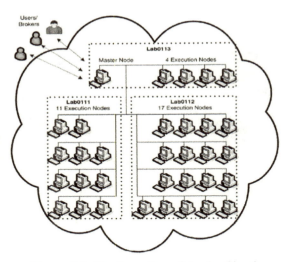

Figure 2.6: Configuration of Aneka Cloud

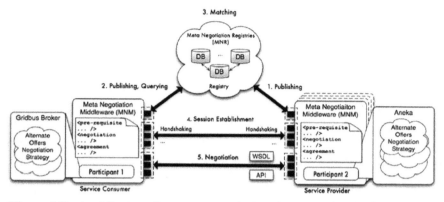

Figure 2.7: Architecture for meta-negotiations between Aneka Clouds and clients

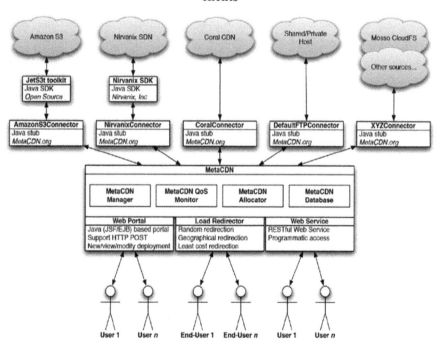

Figure 2.8: The MetaCDN (Content Delivery Network) system

2.1.2.2. Some Definition and trends

In order to facilitate a clear understanding of what exactly is Cloud computing, we compare Cloud computing with two other recent, widely-adopted or explored computing paradigms: Cluster Computing and Grid Computing. We first examine the respective definitions of these three paradigms.

Definitions

Clusters: ``A cluster is a type of parallel and distributed system, which consists of a collection of inter-connected stand-alone computers working together as a single integrated computing resource.''

Grids: ``A Grid is a type of parallel and distributed system that enables the sharing, selection, and aggregation of geographically distributed `autonomous' resources dynamically at runtime depending on their availability, capability, performance, cost, and users' quality-of-service requirements."

Cloud: ``A Cloud is a type of parallel and distributed system consisting of a collection of inter-connected and virtualized computers that are dynamically provisioned and presented as one or more unified computing resource(s) based on service-level agreements established through negotiation between the service provider and consumers.''

Clouds appear to be a combination of clusters and Grids. Clouds are clearly next-generation data centers with nodes ``virtualized" through hypervisor technologies such as VMs, dynamically ``provisioned'' on demand as a personalized resource collection to meet a specific service-level agreement, which is established through a ``negotiation''.

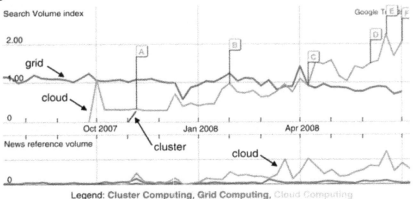

Figure 2.9: Google search trends for year 2007 and 2008.

2.1.3. Case Study3

Ahmad et al. [9] presented a comprehensive analysis of cloud computing. They find the cloud concepts and demonstrate the cloud landscape vendors, growth of cloud computing, user concern about cloud security and worldwide web security

22

revenue 2009 to 2015. They focused on the basic way of cloud computing development, growths and common security issues arising from the usage of cloud services. Their business model is considered to develop our business model.

In this paper, they presented a comprehensive analysis of cloud computing.

They find the cloud concepts and demonstrate the cloud landscape vendors, growth of cloud computing, user concern about cloud security and worldwide web security revenue 2009 to 2015.

In this paper they focused on the basic way of cloud computing development, growths and common security issues arising from the usage of cloud services.

2.1.4. Case Study4

Trancoso and Angeli [10] presented a brief description of GridArchSim, a computer architecture simulation environment that uses a database archive to reduce simulation latency and the Grid platform to increase the throughput of the simulations. This system is still under implementation. The system is going to be used for both research and education.

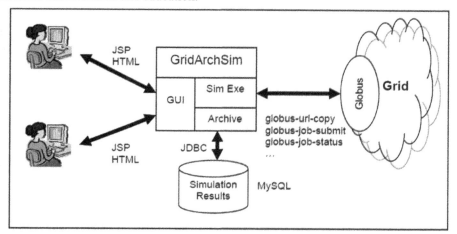

Figure 2.10: Architecture of GridArchSim system.

GUI: The GUI module in GridArchSim is a web-based fully configurable module that is used to provide the user with an interface to the system.

Archive Module: The archive module consists of a database that stores simulation results along with the input parameters used to obtain those results. The current implementation is based on the MySQL database management system and its access is performed using queries on JSP pages.

Simulation Execution Module: Upon a request for simulation, request is submitted to the Grid system for execution which provides both high-availability and high-throughput. The submission of the work to the Grid is done in three steps using the Globus middleware.

Consequently the first step is the one where the system is responsible to send these large files from the client to the host.

In the second step, the execution is spawned on a node on the Grid system.

The third and final step is the one where the system needs to poll the host in order to find if the execution has completed and if the output file may be stored into the database system.

2.1.5. Case Study5

In this work,[11] they presented EUCALYPTUS – an open source software framework for cloud computing that implements what is commonly referred to as Infrastructure as a Service (IaaS); systems that give users the ability to run and control entire virtual machine instances deployed across a variety physical resources.

They outlined the basic principles of the EUCALYPTUS design, detail important operational aspects of the system, and discuss architectural trade-offs that they have made in order to allow Eucalyptus to be portable, modular and simple to use on infrastructure commonly found within academic settings.

Finally, they provided evidence that EUCALYPTUS enables users familiar with existing Grid and HPC systems to explore new cloud computing functionality while maintaining access to existing, familiar application development software and Grid middle-ware.

EUCALYPTUS employs a hierarchical design shown in figure 2.11 to reflect underlying resource topologies. The relationships and deployment locations of each component within a typical small cluster setting are shown in below figure. Each EUCALYPTUS VM instance is assigned a virtual interface that is connected to software Ethernet Bridge on the physical machine, to which a VLAN tagged interface is further connected.

EUCALYPTUS includes Walrus, shown in figure2.12 a S3 compatible storage management service for storing and accessing user data as well as images.

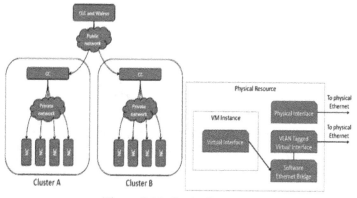

Figure 2.11: Basic Concepts

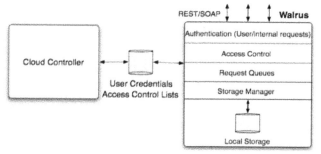

Figure 2.12: EUCALYPTUS includes Walrus, a S3 compatible storage management service for storing and accessing user data as well as images.

Chapter-3

3. Implementation Preparation

3.1. Comparative Study between the Cloud Service Providers

3.1.1. Open Source Advantages

- Leverage the work of a growing community of developers.
- Works across multiple hardware infrastructure.
- Possible to deploy at service providers and on-premise.
- Customized to fit individual needs or to add additional services.

3.1.2. Amazon Web Services

AWS is a collection of remote computing services that together make up a cloud computing platform, offered over the Internet by Amazon.com.

AWS is located in 8 geographical 'Regions': US East, US West, US West, São Paulo, Ireland, Singapore, Tokyo and Sydney.

Availability Zones are isolated from each other to prevent outages from spreading between Zones. Several services operate across Availability Zones while others can be configured to replicate across Zones to spread demand and avoid downtime from failures.

3.1.3. Windows Azure

Windows Azure is a cloud computing platform and infrastructure, created by Microsoft, for building, deploying and managing applications and services through a global network of Microsoft-managed datacenters. It provides both platform as a service (PaaS) and infrastructure as a service (IaaS) services and supports many different programming languages, tools and frameworks, including both Microsoft-specific and third-party software and systems.

3.1.4. Eucalyptus

Eucalyptus is open source software for building Amazon Web Services (AWS)-compatible private and hybrid clouds. It allows an organization to build self-service, elastic clouds inside its datacenter using existing IT infrastructure.

Written in: Java, C

Operating system: Linux, can host Linux and Windows VMs

Platform: Hypervisors (Xen, KVM, VMware)

Cloud Computing Tools:

Cloud computing	
Applications	Web browsers . Google Apps . ownCloud . Microsoft Online . Salesforce .
Platforms	Amazon . App Engine . GreenQloud . AppScale . Windows Azure . Engine Yard . Heroku . OrangeScape .
Infrastructure	Amazon . CloudStack . Eucalyptus . GreenQloud . Google Storage Nimbus . IBM Smartcloud . Nimbula . OpenStack . OpenNebula .
Technologies	Networking . Cloud database . Web APIs . Virtual appliance .Security . Internet . Virtualization . datacenters .

Figure 3.1: Cloud computing Tools

3.2. Cloudsim

CloudSim: A Framework for Modeling and Simulation of Cloud Computing Infrastructures and Services.

These already wide ecosystem of cloud architectures, along with the increasing demand for energy-efficient IT technologies, demand timely, repeatable, and controllable methodologies for evaluation of algorithms, applications, and policies before actual development of cloud products. Because utilization of real testbeds limits the experiments to the scale of the testbed and makes the reproduction of results an extremely difficult undertaking, alternative approaches for testing and experimentation leverage development of new Cloud technologies.

A suitable alternative is the utilization of simulations tools, which open the possibility of evaluating the hypothesis prior to software development in an environment where one can reproduce tests. Specifically in the case of Cloud computing, where access to the infrastructure incurs payments in real currency, simulation-based approaches offer significant benefits, as it allows Cloud customers to test their services in repeatable and controllable environment free of cost, and to tune the performance bottlenecks before deploying on real Clouds. At the provider side, simulation environments allow evaluation of different kinds of resource leasing scenarios under varying load and pricing distributions. Such studies could aid the providers in optimizing the resource access cost with focus on improving profits. In the absence of such simulation platforms, Cloud customers and providers have to rely either on theoretical and imprecise evaluations, or on try-and-error approaches that lead to inefficient service performance and revenue generation.

3.2.1. Installation of Cloudsim using Apache Ant

1. Download clousim, apache_ant and Java version 1.7.0 .
2. Then Install Java.
3. Extract clousim and apache_ant files on C:\
4. open command prompt.

run>>cmd

5. Set the path for Java and apache_ant,both are set the path on bin directory.

C:\>set path=%path%;.;"c:\Program Files\Java\jdk1.7.0\bin";

C:\> set path=%path%;.;C:\apache-ant-1.9.0\bin;

6. Then set the classpath to cloudsim library files.

C:\> set classpath=%classpath%;.;C:\cloudsim-3.0.2\jars\cloudsim-3.0.2.jar;

C:\cloudsim-3.0.2\jars\cloudsim-3.0.2-sources.jar;C:\cloudsim-

3.0.2\jars\cloudsim-examples-3.0.2.jar;C:\cloudsim-3.0.2\jars\cloudsim-examples-

3.0.2-sources.jar

7. Then goto cloudsim example folder using cd command.

C:\>cd C:\cloudsim-3.0.2\examples

8. Compile example1 program using Javac command.

C:\>javac org/cloudbus/cloudsim/examples/CloudSimExample1.java

9. Then Run CloudSimExample1 using java command

C:\>java org.cloudbus.cloudsim.examples.CloudSimExample1

10.Then Result will come and successfully installed cloudsim on your computer.

3.2.2. JAVA

Java is a programming language and computing platform first released by Sun Microsystems in 1995. There are lots of applications and websites that will not work unless we have Java installed, and more are created every day. Java is fast, secure, and reliable. From laptops to datacenters, game consoles to scientific supercomputers, cell phones to the Internet, Java is everywhere!

Finally we need Java to install and run cloudsim.

3.2.3. Apache Ant

Apache Ant is a Java library and command-line tool whose mission is to drive processes described in build files as targets and extension points dependent upon each other. The main known usage of Ant is the build of Java applications. Ant supplies a number of built-in tasks allowing to compile, assemble, test and run Java applications. Ant can also be used effectively to build non Java applications, for instance C or C++ applications.

More generally, Ant can be used to pilot any type of process which can be described in terms of targets and tasks.

3.2.4. Installation of Cloudsim in Command Prompt

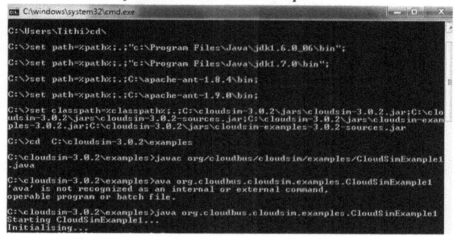

Figure 3.2: Installation of Cloudsim in Command Prompt .

Result of Successful installation of cloudsim on my computer

```
C:\cloudsim-3.0.2\examples>java org.cloudbus.cloudsim.examples.CloudSimExample1
Starting CloudSimExample1...
Initialising...
Starting CloudSim version 3.0
Datacenter_0 is starting...
Broker is starting...
Entities started.
0.0: Broker: Cloud Resource List received with 1 resource(s)
0.0: Broker: Trying to Create UM #0 in Datacenter_0
0.1: Broker: UM #0 has been created in Datacenter #2, Host #0
0.1: Broker: Sending cloudlet 0 to UM #0
400.1: Broker: Cloudlet 0 received
400.1: Broker: All Cloudlets executed. Finishing...
400.1: Broker: Destroying UM #0
Broker is shutting down...
Simulation: No more future events
CloudInformationService: Notify all CloudSim entities for shutting down.
Datacenter_0 is shutting down...
Broker is shutting down...
Simulation completed.
Simulation completed.

=========== OUTPUT ===========
Cloudlet ID    STATUS    Data center ID    UM ID    Time    Start Time    Finish
 Time
    0          SUCCESS         2             0       400      0.1           400.1
*****Datacenter: Datacenter_0*****
User id          Debt
3                35.6
**********************************
CloudSimExample1 finished!

C:\cloudsim-3.0.2\examples>
```

Figure 3.3: Result of Successful installation of cloudsim on my computer.

3.2.5. Cloudsim installation on NetBeans IDE 7.3

NetBeans is an integrated development environment (IDE) for developing primarily with Java, but also with other languages, in particular PHP, C/C++, and HTML5. It is also an application platform framework for Java desktop applications and others. The NetBeans IDE is written in Java and can run on Windows, OS X, Linux, Solaris and other platforms supporting a compatible JVM. The NetBeans Platform allows applications to be developed from a set of modular software components called modules. Applications based on the NetBeans Platform (including the NetBeans IDE itself) can be extended by third party developers.

3.2.6. Java SE Development Kit 7

The JDK is a development environment for building applications, applets, and components using the Java programming language. The JDK includes tools useful for developing and testing programs written in the Java programming language and running on the Java platform.

Step-1

Open Netbeans (any version greater then 5.0) ,Go to file–>>new project

Step-2

select "Java" folder then select first option java Application ,Press next

30

Step-3:

Now give name to the project as you wish , un-check the "create main class" press next.

Setp-4

Now project has been created as shown.

Step-5:

Go to library, right click on it, a menu will come, click on "Add jars/Folders"

Step-6:

Now browse the cloudsim folder which you have extracted from zip file .and go to"cloudsim-2.1.1\jars" and select "cloudsim-2.1.1.jar".

Step-7

Now simply copy the "org" folder in "cloudsim-2.1.1\examples" and paste it to net beans source folder as shown.go to source and right click select paste.

Step-8:

To run the example go to source ->> org.cloudbus.cloudsim.examples->>select any example ,right click on it and select "run" option the output will be displayed in the output window at the bottom.

Output:

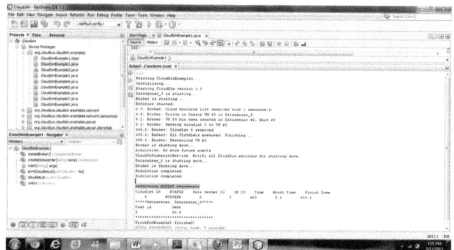

Figure 3.4: Output of running code in NetBeans.

3.3. Openstack

OpenStack is a collection of open source components to deliver public and private IaaS clouds

31

Components: Nova, Swift, Glance, Keystone, and Quantum

IaaS Cloud Services allows users to manage:

VMs, Virtual networks, storage resources

Openstak Installation on Ububtu

3.3.1. *Components of Openstack*

OpenStack has a modular architecture that encompasses following components:

OpenStack Compute (code-name Nova)

OpenStack Object Storage (code-name Swift)

OpenStack Image Service (code-name Glance)

OpenStack Identity (code-name Keystone)

OpenStack Dashboard (code-name Horizon)

OpenStack Networking (code-name Quantum)

OpenStack Block Storage (code-name Cinder)

3.3.3. Installation and Configuration of Openstack on Ububtu:

A minimal cloud infrastructure based on OpenStack can be set up using 3 machines. Server1 runs all the 7 components of Nova as well as Glance and OpenStack dashboard. Server2 runs only nova-compute. Since OpenStack components follow a shared-nothing policy, each component or any group of components can be installed any server.

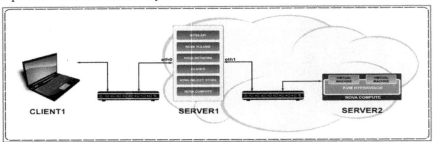

Figure 3.5: Cloud structure.

Table 3.1: Components in different systems.

	Server 1	Server 2	Client 1
Functionality	All components of Open Stack including nova-compute	nova-compute	Client

32

No of NICs	eth0 -Public N/W,eth1 -Private N/W	eth0 -Public N/W,eth1 -Private N/W	eth0- Public N/W
Ip-addresses	Eth0-10.10.10.2,eth1-192.168.3.1	Eth0-10.10.10.3,eth1-192.168.3.2	Eth0-10.10.10.4
Hostname	server1.example.com	server2.example.com	client.example.com
DNS servers	10.10.10.3	10.10.10.3	10.10.10.3
Gateway IP	10.10.10.1	10.10.10.1	10.10.10.1

3.4. Amazon Web Service (AWS)

3.4.1. EC2

Amazon Elastic Compute Cloud (EC2) is a central part of Amazon.com's cloud computing platform, Amazon Web Services (AWS). EC2 allows users to rent virtual computers on which to run their own computer applications. EC2 allows scalable deployment of applications by providing a Web service through which a user can boot an Amazon Machine Image to create a virtual machine, which Amazon calls an "instance", containing any software desired. A user can create, launch, and terminate server instances as needed, paying by the hour for active servers, hence the term "elastic"

3.4.2. S3

Amazon S3 (Simple Storage Service) is an online file storage web service offered by Amazon Web Services. Amazon S3 provides storage through web services interfaces (REST, SOAP, and BitTorrent). Amazon claims that S3 uses the same scalable storage infrastructure that Amazon.com uses to run its own global e-commerce network.

3.4.3. Elastic MapReduce (EMR):

The EMR is a web service that makes it easy to quickly and cost-effectively process vast amounts of data. Amazon EMR uses Hadoop, an open source framework, to distribute data and processing across a resizable cluster of Amazon EC2 instances. We implemented our hadoop on EMR where we experiment the MapReduce function through a number of SQLs by Apache Hive command.

3.4.4. DynamoDB

Amazon DynamoDB is a fully managed NoSQL database service that provides fast and predictable performance with seamless scalability. Amazon DynamoDB enables us to offload the administrative burdens of operating and scaling distributed databases to AWS.

3.5 Technology of Hadoop

Apache Hadoop is an open-source software framework for storing and large scale processing of data-sets on clusters of commodity hardware. Hadoop is an Apache top-level project being built and used by a global community of contributors and users. Pig and Hive are Higher-level languages over Hadoop that generate MapReduce programs. MapReduce is a technique that distributes the processing of very large multi-structured data files across a large cluster of machines. High performance is achieved by breaking the processing into small units of work that can be run in parallel across the hundreds, potentially thousands, of nodes in the cluster. Simple data-parallel programming model designed for scalability and fault-tolerance. The challenges of cheap nodes fail, commodity network, programming distributed systems are solved by building fault-tolerance into system, push computation to the data and data-parallel programming model: users write "map" & "reduce" functions, system distributes work and handles faults. MapReduce programming model hides the complexity of work distribution and fault tolerance. The Principal design philosophies are making it scalable and cheap by lowering hardware, programming and admin costs. MapReduce is not suitable for all problems, but when it works, it saves quite a bit of time. The main features of Hadoop Distributed File System (HDFS) are single namespace for entire cluster and replicates data 3x for fault-tolerance.

3.5.1 Elastic MapReduce (EMR):

The EMR is a web service that makes it easy to quickly and cost-effectively process vast amounts of data. Amazon EMR uses Hadoop, an open source framework, to distribute data and processing across a resizable cluster of Amazon EC2 instances. We implemented our hadoop on EMR where we experiment the MapReduce function through a number of SQLs by Apache Hive command.

Some Features of MapReduce

Pioneered by Google

Processes 20 petabytes of data per day

Popularized by open-source Hadoop project

Where it used for:

- At Google:
  - Index construction for Google Search
  - Article clustering for Google News
  - Statistical machine translation
- At Yahoo!:
  - "Web map" powering Yahoo! Search
  - Spam detection for Yahoo! Mail
- At Facebook:
  - Data mining
  - Ad optimization
  - Spam detection
- In research:
  - Astronomical image analysis (Washington)
  - Bioinformatics (Maryland)
  - Analyzing Wikipedia conflicts (PARC)
  - Natural language processing (CMU)
  - Particle physics (Nebraska)
  - Ocean climate simulation (Washington)

3.5.2. Apache Hive

Apache Hive is a data warehouse infrastructure built on top of Hadoop for providing data summarization, query, and analysis. While initially developed by Facebook, Apache Hive is now used and developed by other companies such as Netflix. Amazon maintains a software fork of Apache Hive that is included in Amazon Elastic MapReduce on Amazon Web Services.

3.5.3. HortonWorks

The Hortonworks Data Platform [21] is a framework that allows for the distributed processing of large data sets across clusters of computers. It includes Apache Hadoop and is used for storing, processing, and analyzing large volumes of data. The platform is designed to deal with data from many sources and formats. The platform includes various Apache Hadoop projects including the Hadoop Distributed File System, MapReduce, Pig, Hive, HBase and Zookeeper and additional components. In our current experiment we implemented the remote cloud through EMR but in case of the implementation of our hybrid cloud we would need a framework like Hortonworks Data Platform. So, we also implemented HDP [21] using four nodded cluster where one was head node using four other EC2 instances. In following part we only will discuss the result based on EMR.

3.5.4. Typical Hadoop Cluster:

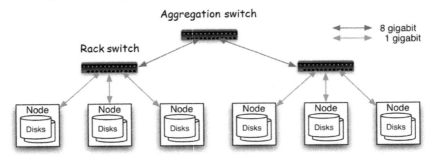

Figure 3.6: Typical Hadoop cluster..

40 nodes/rack, 1000-4000 nodes in cluster

1 Gbps bandwidth within rack, 8 Gbps out of rack

Node specs (Yahoo terasort): 8 x 2GHz cores, 8 GB RAM, 4 disks (= 4 TB?)

3.5.5. Challenges:

- Cheap nodes fail, especially if we have many
o Mean time between failures for 1 node = 3 years
o Mean time between failures for 1000 nodes = 1 day
o Solution: Build fault-tolerance into system
- Commodity network = low bandwidth
o Solution: Push computation to the data
- Programming distributed systems is hard
o Solution: Data-parallel programming model: users write "map" & "reduce" functions, system distributes work and handles faults .

3.5.6. Principal design philosophies

MapReduce programming model hides the complexity of work distribution and fault tolerance

Principal design philosophies:

Make it scalable, so you can throw hardware at problems

Make it cheap, lowering hardware, programming and admin costs

MapReduce is not suitable for all problems, but when it works, it may save you quite a bit of time

Cloud computing makes it straightforward to start using Hadoop (or other parallel software) at scale

3.5.7. Hadoop Components:
- **Distributed file system (HDFS)**
- – Single namespace for entire cluster
- – Replicates data 3x for fault-tolerance
- **MapReduce framework**
- – Executes user jobs specified as "map" and "reduce" functions
- – Manages work distribution & fault-tolerance

3.5.8. Hadoop Distributed File System
- Files split into 128MB *blocks*
- Blocks replicated across several *datanodes* (usually 3)
- Single *namenode* stores metadata (file names, block locations, etc)

- Optimized for large files, sequential reads
- Files are append-only

Figure 3.7: Nodes of Hadoop.

Chapter-4

4. ARCHITECTURE OF HYBRID STRUCTURED CLOUD

We considered national ID database for searching Bangladeshi People in different purpose. An interactive web based application prototype by using hybrid structure of cloud computing has implemented in our research. This is based on Hadoop with HortonWorks Data Platform (HDP) for local cloud structure. We used four elastic (EC2) nodes that are installed on Amazon Web Service (AWS). All the nodes including the head node is implemented on CentOS verstion-6.3 operating system. To address the authentication we also enabled public key and private key tool. Hadoop is an open-source software framework that supports data-intensive distributed applications. Hadoop implements a computational paradigm named map-reduce [13], where the application is divided into many small fragments of work, each of which may be executed or re-executed on any node in the cluster. Amazon EMR uses

37

Hadoop, an open source framework, to distribute data and processing across a resizable cluster of Amazon EC2 instances. We implemented our hadoop on EMR where we experiment the MapReduce function through a number of SQLs by Apache Hive command for our remote cloud.

4.1. Structural Description

In our research we proposed a hybrid structure of cloud computing as depicted in figure 4.1. This structure is divided into two parts. One infrastructure will be locally implemented by using "Eucalyptus" and the other part of the infrastructure will be implemented in well-known Amazon Web Service (AWS) cloud. On top of this infrastructure Hadoop framework would be used to implement the system. In our structure the solid lined servers are representing the "always on" server. In local elastic cloud part those servers will be used for query handling requested by the users and in External AWS cloud those server will be used for backup and mirroring. In local elastic cloud part dashed line servers will be used as elastic computer which will be automatically "UP" as needs' basis. The number of server will depend on the number of query request. In External AWS cloud the dashed server will be used is case of overflow request and in case of local cloud infrastructure failure. Any kind of Linux server can be used for this implementation. We used CentOS in our prototype cloud and Hadoop implementation. [25], [24] HiveQL is the preferable database for our proposed system but we used MySQL for our prototype. Different type of devices around Local Elastic Cloud indicates that our system would support entire computing platform.

To implement Local cloud using AWS HortonWorks data platform is used and experimented this is shown in this chapter. We used Debian Linux in our prototype cloud (EMR) and Hadoop implementation in next chapter.

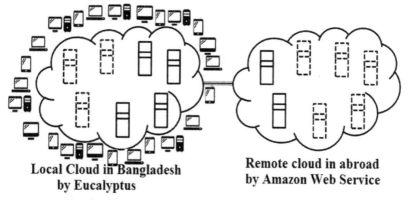

**Local Cloud in Bangladesh
by Eucalyptus**

**Remote cloud in abroad
by Amazon Web Service**

Figure 4.1: Block Diagram of BDPS System

Figure 4.2 is showing the architecture of our proposed BDPS system. It shows that the Database is stored in the hybrid cloud which is made by Local and Remote cloud. Hadoop framework contains both structure and the Database. Data input authority and User can access this database by a user interface which is connected to Hadoop with secured communication protocol. The selection criteria for local and remote cloud are also shown in our architecture.

4.2. Technology of implementation

An open-source software framework Apache Hadoop [15] supports data distributed applications. In this framework large and segmented hardware is used to run an application. It also supports commodity hardware infrastructure. Hadoop provides reliable data motion to all of its applications. This framework implements map-reduce [13] computational paradigm. In map-reduce paradigm, an application is divided into many small pieces of work and they are distributed to the nodes in the cluster for execution. Pig and Hive are Higher-level languages over Hadoop that generate MapReduce programs .In addition, Hadoop provides a distributed file system that stores data on the compute nodes, providing very high aggregate bandwidth across the cluster. Map-reduce and the distributed file systems are not only designed for running the application efficiently but also to handle node failures automatically. Typical hadoop cluster is shown in figure 4.3.

The challenges of cheap nodes fail, commodity network, programming distributed systems are solved by building fault-tolerance into system, push computation to the data and data-parallel programming model: users write "map" & "reduce" functions, system distributes work and handles faults. MapReduce programming model hides the complexity of work distribution and fault tolerance. The main principal of this design is to make the system scalable and cheap. The main features of Hadoop Distributed File System (HDFS) are single namespace for entire cluster and replicates data 3x for fault-tolerance.

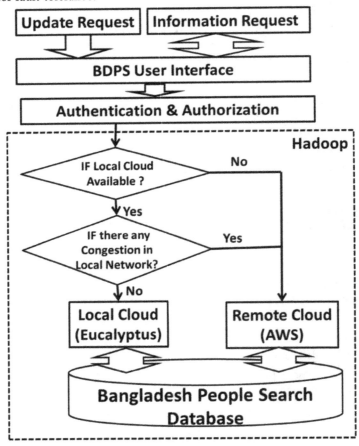

Figure 4.2: Architecture of BDPS System

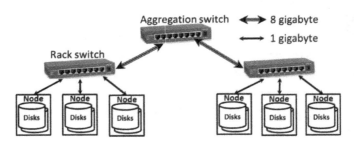

Figure 4.3: Typical hadoop cluster

The Hortonworks Data Platform [21] is a framework to implement Apache Hadoop. The platform includes various Apache Hadoop projects including the Hadoop Distributed File System, MapReduce, Pig, Hive, HBase and Zookeeper and many other additional components. The platform is designed to deal with big data from many sources and formats.

The National ID database of Bangladesh contains 31 information of voter which includes picture and figure print. The total number of voter is almost 95 million on November, 2013. National ID number of Bangladesh contains 13 digits. The structure is "DDRTTUUSSSSSS". "DD" is using for District code, "R" for R.M.O code, "TT" for Thana code, "UU" for Union code and the last "SSSSSS" six digits are a unique number for each citizen of the country. Figure 4.4 is showing a sample of national ID card.

Figure 4.4: Sample of National ID card of Bangladesh

For handling this huge database, an interactive web based application is proposed using hybrid structure of cloud computing. A prototype of this infrastructure has implemented in our research which is based on [14] Hadoop with [20] HortonWorks Data Platform (HDP). We used four elastic (EC2) nodes that are installed on Amazon Web Service (AWS). [19] All the nodes including the head node is implemented on CentOS verstion-6.3 operating system. To address the authentication we also enabled public key and private key tool. This system contains entire tools of hadoop which is shown in Figure 4.5. We discuss some of components in next part of our discussion related of this frame work.

Figure 4.5: Four Nodes having Hadoop Components

4.3. Implementation on AWS

4.3.1. AWS and EC2 Configuration

Registration Procedure

- Registration
- Try to get services
- But did not get because of Credit card registration
- Applied Education Grants Program
- Approved 100$ for 1 year
- Try to get services
- But did not get because of Credit card registration
- Requested AWS without credit card registration
- But they refused
- Tried with BRAC Bank Credit card
- But got error while confirming the payment. They wanted to charge 1$ for verification but bank did not authorize the payment.
- Call bank to know about the authorization
- According to the instruction Endorsed dollar in my credit card
- Requested Bank to authorize the online transection for education purpose
- Request Amazon support center to try payment confirmation again
- Request Amazon education grant program authority
- After this long process Finally got the access to the AWS Service

42

Signup for EC2

- Sign Up for EC2
- Launch a Windows Instance
- Retrieve Password
- Connecting to Amazon EC2 Windows Instances
- Reff: http://docs.aws.amazon.com

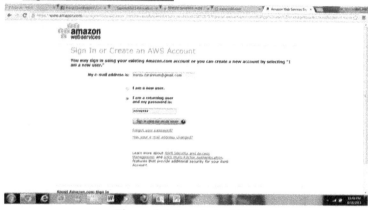

Figure 4.6: Log in to AWS

Figure 4.7: AWS Services

Lunch EC2 Instance

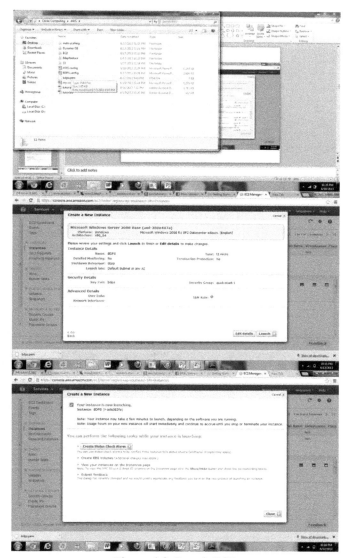

Figure 4.8: Lunch EC2

45

Instance Running

Figure 4.9: Log in to AWS

Password Retrieve

Figure 4.10: Password retrieve

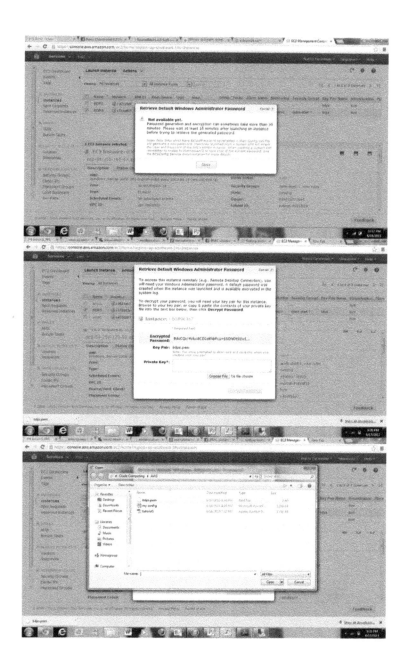

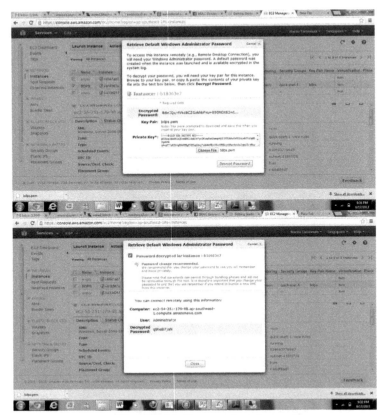

Figure 4.11: Password retrive

Remote Desktop Connection

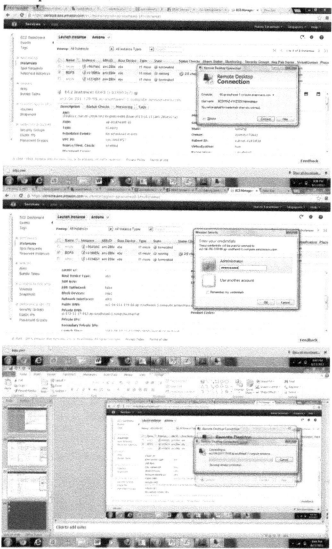

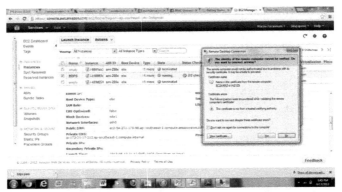

Figure 4.12: Connect from Windows PC

DNS: ec2-54-251-161-47.ap-southeast-1.compute.amazonaws.com

- Name: Administrator
- Password: geqjCJ!M?zy
- We need to install Java on the cluster machines in order to run Hadoop. The OpenJDK7 will suffice for this tutorial. Connect to all three machines using Putty or mRemote, and on **each** of the three machines run the following:

    sudo apt-get install openjdk-7-jdk

- When that's complete, configure the JAVA_HOME variable by adding the following line at the top of ~/.bashrc:

    export JAVA_HOME=/usr/lib/jvm/java-7-openjdk-amd64/

- We can now download and unpack Hadoop. On **each** of the three machines run the following:

    cd ~

    wget   http://mirrors.ispros.com.bd/apache/hadoop/common/hadoop-
    1.1.2/hadoop-1.1.2-bin.tar.gz

    gzip –d hadoop-1.1.2-bin.tar.gz

    tar –xf hadoop-1.1.2-bin.tar

Figure 4.13: Remote Windows Desktop

- Windows Computer:
  - Computer: ec2-54-218-36-242.us-west-2.compute.amazonaws.com
  - Username: Administrator
  - Password: TzNygSiy8F
- Ubuntu:
  - ec2-54-218-30-117.us-west-2.compute.amazonaws.com

Installed Components

- **For JAVA**
  - **JDEJava JDK7**
  - **NetBeans IDE 7.3.1**
  - **Dr. Java**
  - **Ecelipse**
- **7Zip**
- **For PHP**
  - **Microsoft Visual C++ 2008 SP1 Redistributable Package (x86)**
  - **XAMPP**
    - **Apache 2.4.3**
    - **MySQL 5.5.27**
    - **PHP 5.4.7**
    - **phpMyAdmin 3.5.2.2**

- **FileZilla FTP Server 0.9.41**
- **Tomcat 7.0.30 (with mod_proxy_ajp as connector)**
- **Strawberry Perl 5.16.1.1 Portable**
- **XAMPP Control Panel 3.1.0 (from hackattack142)**
- **Download older versions of XAMPP (even the "old" WAMPP) directly from <u>SourceForge</u>.**

4.4. Install Hadoop with HortonWorks Data Platform (HDP)

In following part, we will discuss Hadoop installetion with HortonWorks Data Platform. We implemented it using AWS EC2 infra-structure. Four instances with CentOS version 6.3 are used as the platform which will perform as a parallel distributed system. In those four nodes one was head node. Since we were working with windows environment, we used terminal emulator "putty" for configuring all those nodes, which enabled all those machines to access individually and parallel distributed way. For example if we give a command like **"pdsh -a whoami"**, all four machines will execute this instruction in the same time. Preparing nodes in cluster we downloaded and installed Apache Ambari server which enabled us to work with hadoop. We installed Hortonworks Management Center (HMC) on this server and configure its authentication to install hadoop from windows platform.

After configuring all this things we could install and configure hadoop in these four node computing cluster. We can install this by login from a remote computer by using any kind of web browser. We had to assign master components to the hosts which include NameNode, SNameNode, JobTracker, Nagious Server, Ganglia Collector, Hive Metastore, WebHCat Server, HBase Master, Oozie Server and ZooKeeper. This assignment is not always constant. We can choose according to our requirement. After completing successful hadoop installation we can observe and log the performance and activity from any web browser.

4.4.1. Setting up EC2

*4.4.*1.1 Deploy Instances

AWS Management Console > EC2 Services > Click "**Launch Instance**"

Select a AMI with CentOS 6.x: CentOS6.3_01-02-13 (ami-11733143)

Select 4 instances **Medium** of type **Launch Instance** (instead of spot)

Kernel ID + RAM Disk ID = **Use Default**

Instance Details = **Use DefaultCreate New Key Pair**

1 key pair used for all instances named: **bdps.pem**

1 security group for all 4 instances:

Name group = **hdp-sg1**

Description = security port settings for 4 node cluster HDP installation

Add the rule for **ALL (0.0.0.0/0)** and then save

Click on '**Running Instances**'

4.4.1.2 Connect to EC2 Instances from Windows

Putty: http://www.chiark.greenend.org.uk/~sgtatham/putty/download.html

Required: download Putty in C:\>

Required: download PuttyGen in C:\>

Required: download pscp in C:\>

Create .ppk file for Putty SSH client

Open PuttyGen, and Click Conversions > Import Key

Navigate and select bdps.pem that was created in previous steps.

Click Save, no passphrase, as: bdps.ppk

Get the Public IPs and Public DNSs for all EC2 instance and save in info.txt file
    54.254.183.251

ec2-54-254-183-251.ap-southeast-1.compute.amazonaws.com

54.254.184.25

ec2-54-254-184-25.ap-southeast-1.compute.amazonaws.com

54.254.184.28

ec2-54-254-184-28.ap-southeast-1.compute.amazonaws.com

54.254.184.26

ec2-54-254-184-26.ap-southeast-1.compute.amazonaws.com

Connect to EC2 master instance with Putty

Open Putty; enter the IP address in the Host Name field.

In the category tree to the left, select Connections > Data

In the Auto-login username field put 'root'

In the category tree to the left, select Connections > SSH > Auth

Under Authentication Parameters Private Key File For Authentication

Hit browse, and select bdps.ppk created in the last step

Go back to Session in the category tree to the left

Type a name for this configuration under Saved Sessions, I called mine "bdps"

Figure 4.13: Connect through PiTTY

Click Open to connect to the EC2 instance.

Figure 4.14: Logged in

4.4.2. Setting Up Linux

4.4.2.1 Gather Amazon EC2 Instance Details in info.txt file

4.4.2.2 Initial Head Node Setup

Open Windows Start >> Run: cmd >> EXECUTE Windows Client:

c:\ pscp -i bdps.ppk bdps.pem root@54.254.163.55:/root/.ssh/id_rsa

4.4.2.2.1 Setup Password-less SSH on Head Node

Connect to EC2 master instance with Putty

ls /root/.ssh

chmod 700 /root/.ssh ; chmod 640 /root/.ssh/authorized_keys ; chmod 600 /root/.ssh/id_rsa

4.4.2.2.2 Get Network Configuration For Each Node

echo -e "`hostname -i`\t`hostname -f`\th1"

Save "172.31.20.160   ip-172-31-20-160.us-west-2.compute.internal   h1" in info.txt

ssh 54.254.162.223

[TYPE NO TO AUTHENTICATION REQUEST]

sed   -i   's/^.*StrictHostKeyChecking.*$/StrictHostKeyChecking=no/' /etc/ssh/ssh_config ; service sshd restart

ssh 54.254.162.223

echo -e "`hostname -i`\t`hostname -f`\tn1"

Save IP DNS and node info in info.txt

172.31.6.157   ip-172-31-6-157.ap-southeast-1.compute.internal n1

#exit

ssh 54.254.166.35

echo -e "`hostname -i`\t`hostname -f`\tn2"

Save IP DNS and node info in info.txt

172.31.6.154   ip-172-31-6-154.ap-southeast-1.compute.internal n2

#exit

ssh 54.254.148.228

echo -e "`hostname -i`\t`hostname -f`\tn2"

Save IP DNS and node info in info.txt

172.31.6.155   ip-172-31-6-155.ap-southeast-1.compute.internal n3

#exit

4.4.2.2.3 Setup Head and N1, N2, N3 Hosts File

Copy following addresses in all nodes and Head in hosts file

vi /etc/hosts

KEYBOARD INPUT=lowercase: o

172.31.6.156   ip-172-31-6-156.ap-southeast-1.compute.internal h1
172.31.6.157   ip-172-31-6-157.ap-southeast-1.compute.internal n1
172.31.6.154   ip-172-31-6-154.ap-southeast-1.compute.internal n2
172.31.6.155   ip-172-31-6-155.ap-southeast-1.compute.internal n3

KEYBOARD INPUT=escape

KEYBOARD INPUT=capital: ZZ

ssh n1

vi /etc/hosts

exit

ssh n2

vi /etc/hosts

exit

ssh n3

vi /etc/hosts

exit

4.4.2.2.4 Setup Repository on Head Node

scp /etc/yum.repos.d/CentOS-Base.repo n1:/etc/yum.repos.d/CentOS-Base.repo

scp /etc/yum.repos.d/CentOS-Base.repo n2:/etc/yum.repos.d/CentOS-Base.repo

scp /etc/yum.repos.d/CentOS-Base.repo n3:/etc/yum.repos.d/CentOS-Base.repo

4.4.2.2.5 Setup Repository on Head Node

rpm -Uvh http://s3.amazonaws.com/public-repo-1.hortonworks.com/AMBARI-
1.x/repos/centos6/AMBARI-1.x-1.el6.noarch.rpm

pdsh –a "chmod 700 /root/.ssh ; chmod 640 /root/.ssh/authorized_keys ; chmod
600 /root/.ssh/id_rsa"

pdsh –a "sed -i 's/^.*StrictHostKeyChecking.*$/StrictHostKeyChecking=no/'
/etc/ssh/ssh_config ; service sshd restart"

4.4.2.2.6 Setup pdsh and Configuration File To Execute Commands In Parallel
Across Nodes

yum install -y pdsh

vi /etc/pdsh/machines

pdsh -a whoami

4.4.2.3 Prepare nodes in cluster for installation of Hadoop

CTRL + R rpm

pdsh -a "http://s3.amazonaws.com/public-repo-1.hortonworks.com/AMBARI-
1.x/repos/centos6/AMBARI-1.x-1.el6.noarch.rpm" | dshbak

pdsh -a 'ls /etc/yum.repos.d/' | dshbak

4.4.3. Installing Hadoop

4.4.3.1 Configure Supporting Software & Services

4.4.3.1.1 Check & Remove Dependent Software that is Pre-Installed

rpm -qa | grep -ie ruby -ie passenger -ie nagios -ie ganglia -ie puppet -ie rrdtool -
ie mysql

yum erase -y ruby* rrdtool* epel*

pdsh -a "yum erase -y ruby* rrdtool* epel*"

4.4.3.1.2 Check, Install, and Configure Services

service ntpd status

yum install -y ntp

pdsh -a "yum install -y ntp"

chkconfig ntpd on ; chkconfig iptables off

pdsh -a "chkconfig ntpd on ; chkconfig iptables off"

pdsh -a reboot

 # reboot

service ntpd status ; service iptables status

 # pdsh -a "service ntpd status ; service iptables status" | dshbak

4.4.3.2 Install Hortonworks Management Center (HMC)

yum install -y epel-release

pdsh -a "yum install -y epel-release"

yum install -y ambari-server

ambari-server setup

KEYBOARD INPUT=n

KEYBOARD INPUT=y

ambari-server start

4.4.3.3 Setup Installation Parameters, and Install Hadoop via HMC Installation Wizard

http://54.200.34.142:8080

Login, username & password = admin

Name cluster: "bdps"

Installation Options

We put address of each node and choose the private key file (bdps.pem) being used.

ip-172-31-6-156.ap-southeast-1.compute.internal

ip-172-31-6-157.ap-southeast-1.compute.internal

ip-172-31-6-154.ap-southeast-1.compute.internal

ip-172-31-6-155.ap-southeast-1.compute.internal

Target Hosts

Enter a list of host names, one per line. Or use Pattern Expressions

```
ip-172-31-6-156.ap-southeast-1.compute.internal
ip-172-31-6-157.ap-southeast-1.compute.internal
ip-172-31-6-154.ap-southeast-1.compute.internal
ip-172-31-6-155.ap-southeast-1.compute.internal
```

Host Connectivity Information

☑ Provide your SSH Private Key (id_rsa for root) and use SSH to automatically register hosts

[Choose File] hdp-privkey1.pem

```
-----BEGIN RSA PRIVATE KEY-----
MIIEpAIBAAKCAQEAuPLysGupbhwNyERxZfjN/ee9dNo2gdGanq1wyw1Sa8
TtBoW54PjO+DJX7R5x
NNrqT4LybBGBRfDvFuWx5NKHThxygPy25maUetKCFKz2NqEAmRhyDs+s1r
q+81I11ZMH1Bb/rQiA
g8xaggRzh6f2p1FZetP7ENQ8vEGlZ8SoVwZGgf61moHsa9B3kCMOtTKKZG
LVAr5jKxyrHaonJCtt
PDO7/jI/4eB2tif3Tz4EAhQ2Ir1exPSCHWmr1oFVA2An1kfF0MRfGuBQyy
uqMa+0qdacPJds8ZD7
26B0jB04kChLoZYkiqxTMLf8UVBXqjd5mhPoZJEjTjGf9RrQ1ucQywIDAQ
```

Advanced Options

☐ Use a Local Software Repository instead of downloading software packages from the Internet

☐ Path to 64-bit JDK JAVA_HOME on all hosts

```
/usr/jdk/jdk1.6.0_31
```

Figure 4.15: Configuration of Hortonworks

Chosen Services

Leaved all services checked and clicked 'Select Services'

Assigned Masters / Assigned Slaves & Clients

Leaved this section to the default settings

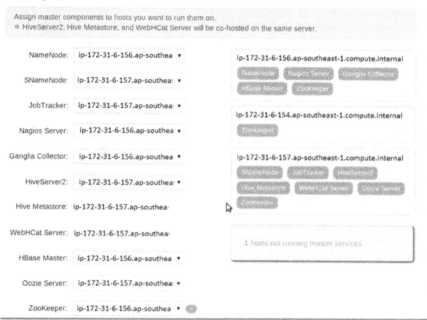

Assign Masters

Assign master components to hosts you want to run them on.
• HiveServer2, Hive Metastore, and WebHCat Server will be co-hosted on the same server.

NameNode:	ip-172-31-6-156.ap-southea ▾
SNameNode:	ip-172-31-6-157.ap-southea: ▾
JobTracker:	ip-172-31-6-157.ap-southea: ▾
Nagios Server:	ip-172-31-6-156.ap-southea ▾
Ganglia Collector:	ip-172-31-6-156.ap-southea ▾
HiveServer2:	ip-172-31-6-157.ap-southea: ▾
Hive Metastore:	ip-172-31-6-157.ap-southea:
WebHCat Server:	ip-172-31-6-157.ap-southea:
HBase Master:	ip-172-31-6-156.ap-southea ▾
Oozie Server:	ip-172-31-6-157.ap-southea: ▾
ZooKeeper:	ip-172-31-6-156.ap-southea ▾

ip-172-31-6-156.ap-southeast-1.compute.internal
NameNode   Nagios Server   Ganglia Collector
HBase Master   ZooKeeper

ip-172-31-6-154.ap-southeast-1.compute.internal
ZooKeeper

ip-172-31-6-157.ap-southeast-1.compute.internal
SNameNode   JobTracker   HiveServer2
Hive Metastore   WebHCat Server   Oozie Server
ZooKeeper

1 hosts not running master services

Figure 4.16: Components Distribution in HDP

Selected Installation Points

Used the default directories

Customized Services

Nagios Tab

Filled-in Nagios Admin Password & Email as "bdps" and narzu.tarannum@gmail.com

Hive/HCat Tab

Filled-in MySQL Password as bdps

Clicked 'Finished customizing all components' and then 'Deploy'

Assign Masters

Assign master components to hosts you want to run them on.
* HiveServer2, Hive Metastore, and WebHCat Server will be co-hosted on the same server.

We have come up with recommended configurations for the services you selected. Customize them as you see fit.

HDFS　　MapReduce　　Hive/HCat **1**　　WebHCat　　HBase　　ZooKeeper　　Oozie　　Nagios **2**

▼ NameNode

NameNode host	ip-172-31-6-156.ap-southeast-1.compute.internal
NameNode directories	/hadoop/hdfs/namenode
NameNode Java heap size	1024　　MB
NameNode new generation size	200　　MB

▼ SNameNode

SNameNode host	ip-172-31-6-157.ap-southeast-1.compute.internal

Figure 4.17: Assign Master node

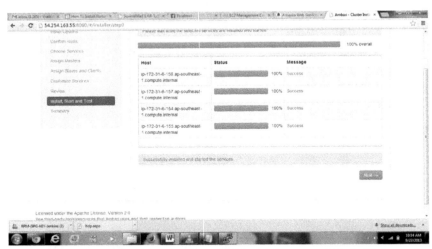

Figure 4.18: Successful Notification from HDP which means 4 Node Hadoop cluster created and installed.

60

Figure 4.19: Hadoop in HDP Summary

Figure 4.20: Cluster load and Network, CPU & memory uses by our four nodes

61

Figure 4.20:Above screenshot is showing the disk space used in presentence

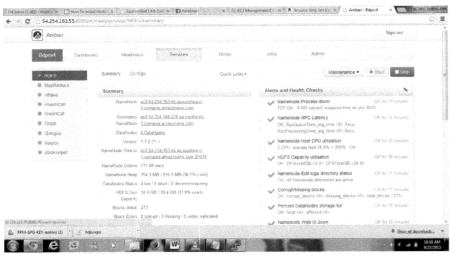

Figure 4.21: Services

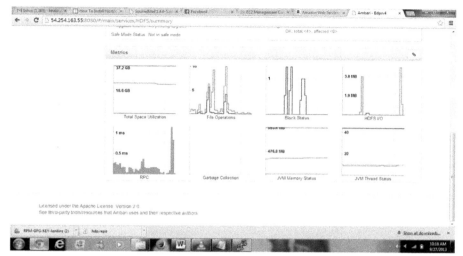

Figure 4.22: Service description used in four nodes.

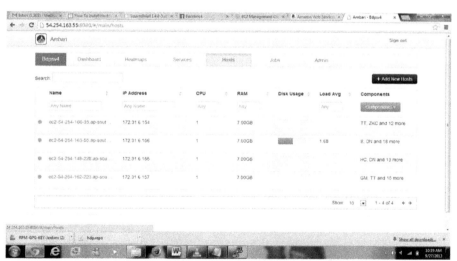

Figure 4.23: Hosts description

Figure 4.24: Jobs description.

Figure 4.25: admin panel of HDP.

4.5.AWS Bill:

Amazon Web Services	Name: Narzu Tarannum
Billing Statement: October 1 - October 31, 2013	Email: narzu.tarannum@gmail.com
Date Printed: October 28, 2013	Account Number: 9396-9377-9943

$0.00 AWS Service Charges
Amazon Elastic Compute Cloud
» $0.00

	EDU_Course_Tarannum_NorthSouthU_09-2013	Credit	-314.13
			-314.13

US West (Oregon) Region
  Amazon EC2 running Linux/UNIX

$0.060 per M1 Standard Small (m1.small) Linux/UNIX instance-hour (or partial hour)	2,596 Hrs	155.76

  Amazon EC2 EBS

$0.10 per 1 million I/O requests	6,371,853 IOs	0.64
$0.10 per GB-month of provisioned storage	34,839 GB-Mo	3.48
		159.88

Asia Pacific (Singapore) Region
  Amazon EC2 running Linux/UNIX

$0.320 per M1 Standard Large (m1.large) Linux/UNIX instance-hour (or partial hour)	469 Hrs	150.08

  Amazon EC2 running Windows

$0.00 per Windows Micro (t1.micro) instance-hour (or partial hour) under monthly free tier	113 Hrs	0.00

  Amazon EC2 EBS

$0.00 per GB-month of provisioned storage under monthly free tier	30,000 GB-Mo	0.00
$0.00 for the first 2 million I/O requests under monthly free tier	2,000,000 IOs	0.00
$0.11 per 1 million I/O requests	6,868,603 IOs	0.76
$0.11 per GB-month of provisioned storage	30.968 GB-Mo	3.41

  Amazon CloudWatch

$0.00 per alarm-month - first 10 alarms	0.872 Alarms	0.00
		154.25

Figure 4.26: Partial Bill of AWS

Credits

Applicable Product(s)	Credits Remaining ($) §
Amazon Route 53, Elastic MapReduce, EC2, SES, SWF, CloudWatch, FWS Lifecycle, Simple Queue Service (BETA), Alexa Web Information Service, AWS Data Transfer, SNS, Redshift, Glacier, Alexa Top Sites, SimpleDB, S3, AWS Storage Gateway, VPC, CloudSearch, ElastiCache, AWS OpsWorks, AWS Direct Connect, DynamoDB, CloudFront, and RDS	$10.00
Amazon Route 53, SES, Elastic MapReduce, EC2, AWS CloudHSM, AWS Data Transfer, Redshift, Glacier, SimpleDB, S3, AWS Storage Gateway, VPC, CloudSearch, ElastiCache, SQS, AWS Elastic Beanstalk, Elastic Transcoder, Basic, AWS Direct Connect, Simple EDI, DynamoDB, AWS Data Pipeline, CloudFront, RDS, and Simple Notification Service	$88.93
Amazon Route 53, SES, Elastic MapReduce, EC2, AWS CloudHSM, AWS Data Transfer, Redshift, Glacier, SimpleDB, S3, AWS Storage Gateway, VPC, CloudSearch, ElastiCache, SQS, AWS Elastic Beanstalk, Elastic Transcoder, Basic, AWS Direct Connect, Simple EDI, DynamoDB, AWS Data Pipeline, CloudFront, RDS, and Simple Notification Service	$300.00
Amazon Route 53, SES, Elastic MapReduce, EC2, AWS CloudHSM, AWS Data Transfer, Redshift, Glacier, SimpleDB, S3, AWS Storage Gateway, VPC, CloudSearch, ElastiCache, SQS, AWS Elastic Beanstalk, Elastic Transcoder, Basic, AWS Direct Connect, Simple EDI, DynamoDB, AWS Data Pipeline, CloudFront, RDS, and Simple Notification Service	$300.00

§ Remaining amounts shown are as of the end of the last statement period (October 1, 2013). Credits will be applied to your account at the close of the statement period.

Figure 4.27: AWS Credits information

Chapter-5

5. Experiment Hadoop with MapReduce

We considered national ID database for searching Bangladeshi People in different purpose. An interactive web based application prototype by using hybrid structure of cloud computing has implemented in our research which is based on Hadoop with EMR. We used four elastic (EC2) nodes that are installed on Amazon Web Service (AWS). EC2 allows users to rent virtual computers on which to run their own computer applications. EC2 allows scalable deployment of applications by providing a Web service through which a user can boot an Amazon Machine Image to create a virtual machine, which Amazon calls an "instance", containing any software desired. Amazon EMR uses Hadoop, an open source framework, to distribute data and processing across a resizable cluster of Amazon EC2 instances. We implemented our hadoop on EMR where we experiment the MapReduce function through a number of SQLs by Apache Hive command. We used Debian Linux in our prototype cloud (EMR) and Hadoop implementation, HiveQL for Database management system. The EMR used four elastic (EC2) nodes that are installed on Amazon Web Service (AWS). All the core nodes including the master node is implemented on large type computing device. To address the authentication we also enabled public key and private key "Keypair" tool of EC2. To log in to any instance, it is mandatory to create a key pair.

This section will discuss the configuration and performance of Hadoop which is implemented on Amazon Elastic MapReduce service [20].

5.1. Lunch Elastic MapReduce (EMR)

After registering with AWS we lunched an Elastic MapReduce cluster which is shown in figure 5.1. The name of our cluster is "BDPS cluster". For lunching we considered following issues:

Figure 5.1 BDPS Elastic MapReduce cluster running in AWS

5.2. BDPS cluster on Amazon MapReduce

5.2.1. Software and Hardware Description

Figure 5.2 is showing the Cluster and Software configuration.

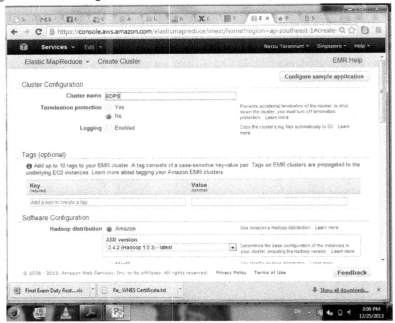

Figure 5.2 Cluster and Software configuration

5.2.2. Software Description

Software configuration is as bellow:

Software	Description
Hadoop distribution	This determines which distribution of Hadoop to run on the cluster. We can choose to run the Amazon distribution of Hadoop or one of several MapR distributions. We have chosen Amazon.
AMI version	This determines the version of Hadoop and other applications such as Hive or Pig to run on the cluster. We selected AMI version 2.4.2 which means Hadoop 1.0.3.
Applications to be installed	A default Hive and Pig version is selected we can also choose other application from the Additional applications list. We did not choose additional applications.

5.2.3. Hardware Description

Following part will discuss hardware configuration where figure 5.3 is showing the configuration:

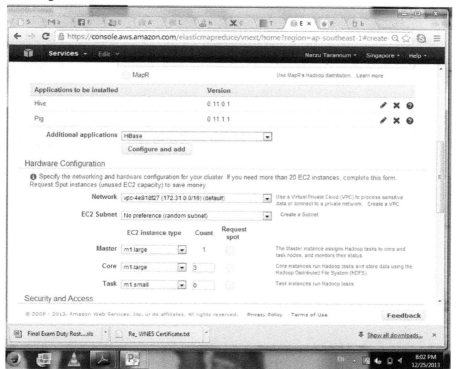

Figure 5.3 Hardware configuration

69

Hardware	Description
Network	Optionally, choose a VPC subnet identifier from the list to launch the cluster in an Amazon VPC. For more information, see Select an Amazon VPC Subnet for the Cluster (Optional) in the Amazon EMR Developer Guide. We choose Launch into EC2-Classic.
Master	The master node assigns Hadoop tasks to core and task nodes, and monitors their status. There is always one master node in each cluster. This specifies the EC2 instance types to use as master nodes. Valid types are m1.small, m1.large, m1.xlarge, c1.medium, c1.xlarge, m2.xlarge, m2.2xlarge, and m2.4xlarge, cc1.4xlarge, cg1.4xlarge. We have chosen m1.large where count was by default 1 which means the number of master node is 1.
Core	A core node is an EC2 instance that runs Hadoop map and reduce tasks and stores data using the Hadoop Distributed File System (HDFS). Core nodes are managed by the master node. This specifies the EC2 instance types to use as core nodes. We have chosen m1.large where the number of core node is 3. This specifies whether to run core nodes on Spot Instances.
Task	Task nodes only process Hadoop tasks and don't store data. You can add and remove them from a cluster to manage the EC2 instance capacity your cluster uses, increasing capacity to handle peak loads and decreasing it later. Task nodes only run a TaskTracker Hadoop daemon. We did not choose any task node in our experiment. This specifies whether to run task nodes on Spot Instances.

5.2.4. EC2 Keypair

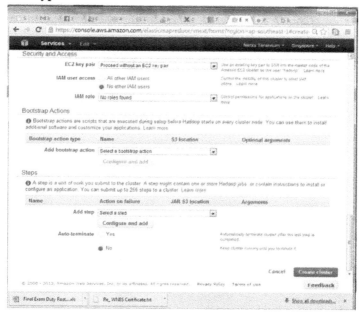

Figure 5.4 Security configuration

Amazon EC2 uses public–key cryptography to encrypt and decrypt login information. Public–key cryptography uses a public key to encrypt a piece of data, such as a password, and then the recipient uses the private key to decrypt the data. The public and private keys are known as a key pair. To log in to any instance, it is mandatory to create a key pair, specifying the name of the key pair when launch the instance, and also need to provide the private key when connect to the instance. Linux/UNIX instances have no password, and can use a key pair to log in using SSH. With Windows instances, can use a key pair to obtain the administrator password and then log in using Remote Desktop Connection. Figure 5.4 is showing the security configuration for BDPS cluster.

5.2.5. Command Line Interface (CLI) by Putty:

PuTTY is a free implementation of Telnet and SSH for Windows and Unix platforms, along with an xterm terminal emulator. Putty allows Windows users to connect to remote systems over the Internet via Telnet and SSH. While both Telnet and SSH allow you to connect to remote systems, SSH, supported in Putty, provides for a "Secure Shell", encrypting information before it is transferred. SSH is an Internet standard, supported by many computers that also support Telnet.

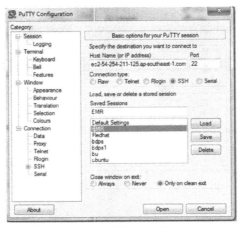

Figure 5.5 PuTTY configuration

Figure 5.5 is showing PuTTY configuration in our implementation, the public domain name of our master node is: ec2-54-254-211-125.ap-southeast-1.compute.amazonaws.com and authentication SSH private key file was bdps.ppk. A PuTTY configuration window in shown in figure 5.5.

5.3. Hadoop and Hive

Figure 5.6 is showing the running of Hadoop and Hive in our PuTTY command line interface. After connecting to the Master node of BDPS cluster we need to write "hadoop" on login prompt. On "Amazon Elastic MapReduce running hadoop" command prompt we have to write "hive" to enter in hive command prompt.

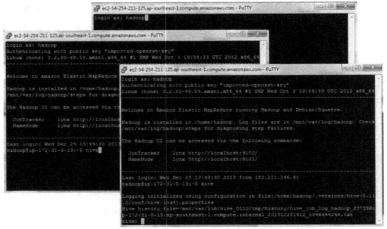

Figure 5.6 Running Hadoop and Hive

5.4. Experiment

We experimented following type of instruction using PuTTY. Since executed the instruction from remote machine to a virtual infra-structure the time of execution varies time to time. So, we counted average time that system had taken. Table 5.1 is showing the time for different types of instructions.

Table 5.1 Experiment Results

Type of Instruction	Total Time	Process Time
Create	0.1205	N/A
Show Table	0.0705	N/A
Select *	0.157	N/A
Drop Table	1.1805	N/A
Load big data from File (3,49,900 words)	0.998	N/A
SQL in Blank Database considering MapReduce	37.1595	0
SQL for small table (3X3 string)	44.235	2.901
SQL in big database for exist data considering MapReduce	44.785	4.915
SQL in big database for non-exist data considering MapReduce	43.8335	4.825

In our table times are showing in Seconds. N/A means it does not involved in MapReduce operation. By this experiment, we found that due to MapReduce operation process time does not vary significantly for big or small database. Process time found almost 3 seconds for very small database and for big database it took less than 5 seconds. A dictionary of 3,49,000 different word is used to experiment big database. Figure 5.7 is showing the output of "show table" and "select *" command with time. Other output windows will be found in appendix-II.

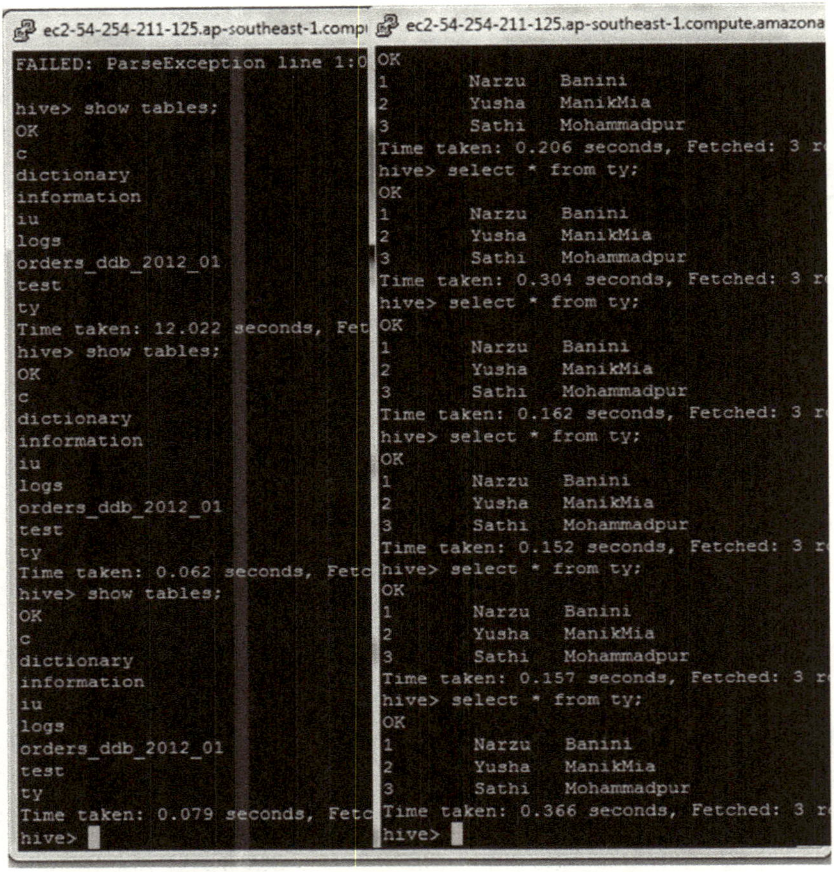

Figure 5.7 Output of "show table" and "select *" command

Chapter-6

6. SYSTEM PROTOTYPE IMPLEMENTATION

We considered national ID database for searching Bangladeshi People in different purpose. An interactive web based application prototype is implemented on Windows 8 server which is lunched as an EC2 instance in AWS. To implement the system we installed XAMPP apache distribution which is an open source web development and hosting package. To design and develop the GUI we used Netbeans IDE6.2.1. We used MySQL for preparing database; PHP is used for Query handling and partial GUI development. HTML is also used to modify the pages. To experiment our system on local host we need to run the XAMPP control panel and start Apache and MySQL modules. To address the authentication and authorization issue and make EC's Database in more effective, efficient and useful, we consider following ideas:

1. Everyone will have a password to access their information and take a printout in a specific format to use in official purpose.

2. Everyone can only check others information by entering info.

3. Academic, Job information, Criminal record can be entered and verified by same database.

6.1. Future of BDPS

BDPS will make the database available to the general people by using the public cloud. Here Election Commission or a National Data Centre will be the service provider. These services are free for General people to access their information. Election Commission or a National Data Centre can introduce a fee for new registration and update process. Since a number of agencies will use this database, a huge amount of revenue is also possible. BDPS will also offer a pay-per-use model for the corporate user who will use this database frequently for information verification.

BDPS own and operate the infrastructure and offer access only via Internet. 3G internetwork will be available in almost everywhere. So, this service would be visible in every mobile device and would be popular with in very short time.

6.2. Service Model for BDPS

Since PaaS helped to run the application on the web and also provide application development toolkits, we choose PaaS as a service model for BDPS. The user of BDPS does not manage or control the underlying cloud infrastructure including network, servers, operating systems, or storage, but has control over the deployed applications.

One important issue in our application was the visibility. Since it is general software and everyone have access to this database, visibility of other's information became an important issue. A unique solution is proposed and implemented to address this issue in our research as follow: 1. everyone will have a password to access their information and take a printout in a specific format to use in official purpose, 2. everyone can only verify other's information by entering known information and 3. Academic, Job information, Income tax, Criminal record can be entered and verified.

6.3. DATABASE

In our prototype, we used five tables for five kinds of data. Our current election commission [22] stores 31 information's for each voter. We kept all those data in information table. Academic Information, Job Record, Bank Account information and Criminal Record stored in other four tables. We implemented our prototype database on MySQL. Tables 1 is showing the name of fields for corresponding tables which is based on the Voter ID application form of election commission Bangladesh shown in Figure 6.1. Partial structures of entire database tables are shown in Figure 8. Bold-italic field means primary key in the figure.

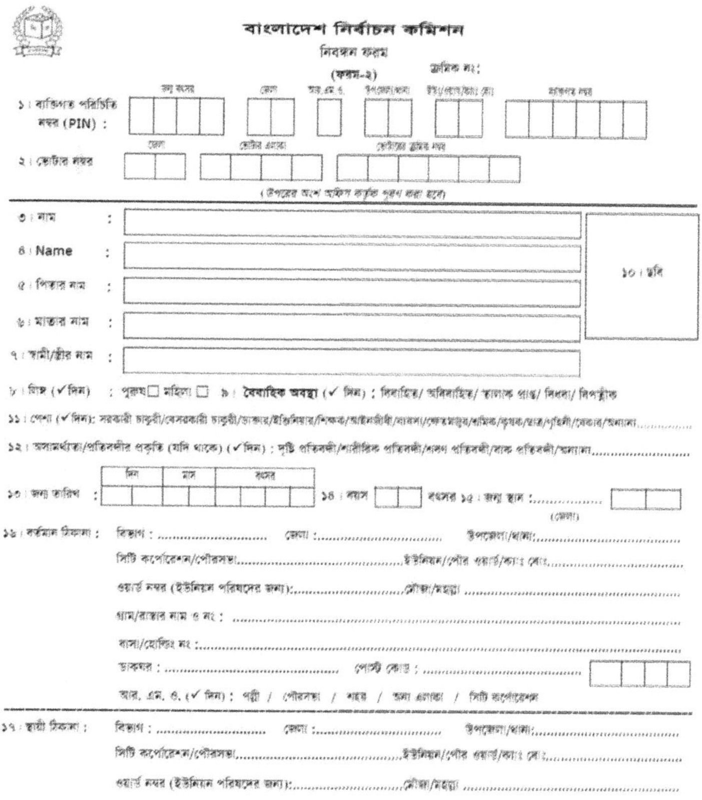

Figure 6.1 Application form of Election Commission

information			
Column	**Type**	**Column**	**Type**
DID	int(11)	Voter_ID	varchar(50)
PIN_ID	varchar(20)	Name	varchar(50)

job_record			education		
Column	**Type**		**Column**	**Type**	
Job_ID	int(11)		*Education_ID*	int(11)	
National_ID	varchar(20)		National_ID	varchar(20)	
Job_title	varchar(20)		Degree_name	varchar(20)	

bank_acc_loan			criminal_record		
Column	**Type**		**Column**	**Type**	
Bank_ID	int(11)		*Record_ID*	int(11)	
National_ID	varchar(20)		National_ID	varchar(20)	
Account_name	varchar(50)		Record_no	varchar(20)	

Figure 6.2 GUIs for information verification

Table 1: FIELDS OF DATABASE.

Table Name	Fields
Information	DID, PIN_ID, Voter_ID, Name, English_name, Father_name, Mother_name, Spouse_name, Gender, Merital_status, Picture, Qualification, Special, Date_of_birth, Birth_district, Present_address, Permanent_address, Voter_area,,Occupation, Specification_sign, B_group, TIN, License, Passport, IRIS_DNA, Phone, Nationality, F_print, Death_date
criminal_record	Record_ID, National_ID, Record_no, Case_no, Type, Place, Police_station, Date, Status, Details
bank_acc_loan	Bank_ID, National_ID, Account_name, Bank_name, Branch_name, Account_no, Card_no, Account_type, Date, Remarks
Education	Education_ID, National_ID, Degree_name, Year, Registration_no, Roll_no, Result, Marks, Remarks
job_record	Job_ID, National_ID, Job_title, Institute, Address, Designation, Joining_date, Departure _date, Remarks

6.4. Web Page Development and Hosting
XAMPP

XAMPP is a very easy to install Apache Distribution for Linux, Solaris, Windows and Mac OS X. The package includes the Apache web server, MySQL, PHP, Perl, a FTP server and phpMyAdmin.

Type: Dynamic

Database: MySQL

Web Development Tools: HTML, PHP

Hosting: Apache Server

XAMPP Control Panel: Start Apache and My SQL

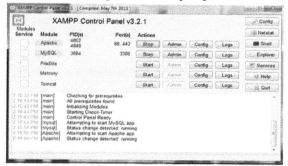

Figure 6.3 XAMPP control Panel

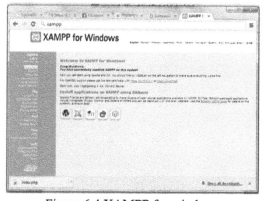

Figure 6.4 XAMPP for windows

6.4.1 Databases:

In our system we have 5 database tables. Figure 6.5 is showing the attributes of our database.

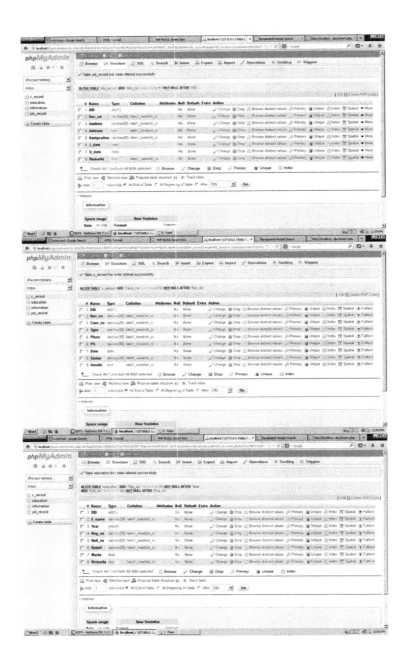

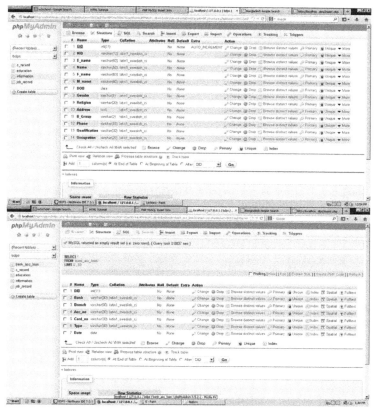

Figure 6.5 Tables with attributes

6.5. SOME SAMPLE SQLs

6.5.1. Insertion Query

We used PHP for entire SQL operations. SQL for Insertion information in the table which PHP code is similar for all other tables:

```
$sql="INSERT INTO information (DID, NID, E_name, Name, F_name, M_name, . . . , Religion)

VALUES

(NULL, '$_POST[nid]', '$_POST[ename]', '$_POST[name]', '$_POST[fname]',
'$_POST[mname]' , . . . , '$_POST[religion]')";
```

6.5.2. Partial SQL for data verification

```php
$result = mysqli_query($con, "SELECT * FROM information WHERE NID='$_POST[nid]'");

while ($row = mysqli_fetch_array($result))

{ echo "For the National ID:"; echo $row['NID']; echo "<br>"; echo "<br>"; echo "<br>"; echo
"Name:  "; echo $_REQUEST["ename"];

  if ($_REQUEST["ename"] == $row['E_name']) {

    echo ".......OK";

  }else { echo "XXXXXXXXXX...Wrong"; }
echo "<br>"; echo "Name in Bangla:  "; echo $_REQUEST["name"];

  if ($_REQUEST["name"] == $row['Name']) {

    echo ".......OK";

  } else {echo "XXXXXXXXXX...Wrong"; }
echo "<br>"; echo "Name in Bangla:  "; echo $_REQUEST["name"];

  if ($_REQUEST["f_name"] == $row['F_name']) {

    echo ".......OK";

  } else {echo "XXXXXXXXXX...Wrong"; }
echo "<br>"; echo "Name in Bangla:  "; echo $_REQUEST["name"];

  if ($_REQUEST["m_name"] == $row['M_name']) {

    echo ".......OK";

  } else {echo "XXXXXXXXXX...Wrong"; }

......

......

echo "<br>";echo "Religion:  "; echo $_REQUEST["religion"];

  if ($_REQUEST["religion"] == $row['Religion']) {

    echo ".......OK";

  } else { echo "XXXXXXXXXX...Wrong";}
  echo "<br>"; }
```

6.6. GUIs

For our prototype we developed 5 GUIs for data entry, 1 GUI for partial data verification for information table and a GUI for checking information. Our GUIs are written in PHP. The list of PHP codes written in Netbeans is showing in Figyre 6.7. Figure 6.6 is the interface of entering data. We have shown a partial record which we entered in the database. By the second GUI we checked with some valid and invalid information and third GUI shows the response of information verification. By this concept we can ensure the visibility of private information from others.

(a) Showing the data entry from with a valid data.

(b) Showing verification from where some data are correct and some are incorrect.

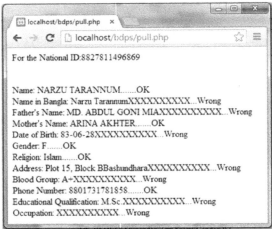

(c) Showing ...OK for correct data and Showing ...Wrong for incorrect data.

Figure 6.6 GUIs for information verification

Figure 6.3 List of php codes in Netbeans

Appendix-I contains all other GUIs and HTML and/or PHP code for this prototype system. SQLs will also found in appendix-I.

Chapter-7

7. Summary

The remote cloud of our proposed hybrid structure is justified with the experiment of Hadoop by EMR of AWS and the Local cloud is justified with the implementation of HDP. This is a reliable and fault-tolerant system because of the characteristic of Hadoop. The main features of Hadoop Distributed File System (HDFS) are single namespace for entire cluster and replicates data 3x for fault-tolerance. We observed that the volume of data does not affect the process time significantly. We experimented a dictionary database with 3,49,000 different word and performed several HiveQL queries for that. We also experimented with some small database and found that the process time does not vary too much. So, if we use big database by increasing the number of elastic node, our system will perform efficiently. BDPS is used here as an example prototype with some unique features.

7.1 Evaluation

According to our proposal and considering the socio-economical aspect, we are expecting 100 thousand request per day in first year, 0.5 million request per day in 3nd year which will touch 1 million marks after five years' service. We projected these numbers by mainly considering the literacy rate of Bangladesh. We also considered that in first few years' educational information, Job information and police record would be incomplete. Since the volume will be increased after every year, we would send the record in different backup file after death. So after 5 years the database volume will come to a stable position.

According to our projection, our local systems would be deployed on a 20-node cluster [27][13]. Each node would have a single 2.40 GHz Intel Core 2 Duo processor. 64-bit CentOS Linux (kernel version 6.3) would be used as Operating System. 4GB RAM with two 250GB SATA-I hard disks would be used as memory and storage. The nodes would be connected with Cisco Catalyst 3750E-48TD switches. The switches are linked together via Cisco StackWise Plus, which creates a 64Gbps ring between the switches.

To justify our proposal we have implemented and experimented with many tools of cloud computing. At the beginning we had simulated a cloud on [19] Cloudsim then we deployed Openstack and experiment some applications for performance study. After that we registered and experimented a number of applications in AWS which includes many kind of EC2 instances, S3 buckets, EMRs, DynamoDB etc. We lunched different type of instances like Windows, CentOS, Ubuntu etc. in different types of machine configurations. Using AWS service we deployed Hadoop with Debian Large machine on four node computing environment on EMR for our remote cloud. Hadoop was experimented on this infer-structure. Using AWS service we also deployed Hadoop with HortonWorks Data Platform (HDP) on four node computing environment on Apache Ambari Server, which we consider for our local cloud. Hortonworks big database was studied on this infer-structure. And lastly we implemented our prototype windows apache server and verified the data entry, visibility and authentication.

7.2 Discussion:

Large scale data handling is a major challenge in Bangladesh. Election commission (EC) of Bangladesh has a national database with 31 types of information for 95 million of voters. Huge cost is involved to maintaining this database which is supposed to use only at the time of election. Considering this point we proposed an application which would be useful to general people, government and non-government organizations along with EC. It will not only ensure the validity of data but also ensure the transparency. We proposed hybrid architecture with map reduce feature for a big database handling application. According to our proposal we can deploy the system on our own local cloud and can synchronize our data with remote cloud. We experimented our proposed hybrid architecture with map reduce feature for a big database. We found that due to MapReduce operation process time does not vary significantly for big or small database. So, this experiment proves that we can deploy the system according to our proposal. It is already justified that our architecture is efficient and fall tolerant. Service we proposed is "pay per use" which would support financially to maintain the database. The data and database is controllable and expandable according to the system's requirement.

References:

[1] Narzu Tarannum and Nova Ahmed, "Efficient and Reliable Hybrid Cloud Architecture for big Database", International Journal on Cloud Computing: Services and Architecture (IJCCSA) ,Vol.3, No.6, December 2013, pp. 17-29, ISSN 2231 - 6663.

[2] Narzu Tarannum and Nova Ahmed, "Hybrid Cloud Infrastructure to Handle Large Scale Data for Bangladesh People Search (BDPS)", 3rd International Conference on Informatics, Electronics & Vision (ICIEV) sponsored by IEEE.

[3] Rajkumar Buyyaa, Chee Shin Yeo, Srikumar Venugopal, James Broberg and Ivona Brandic, "Cloud computing and emerging IT platforms: Vision, hype, and reality for delivering computing as the 5th utility", Future Generation Computer Systems 25 (2009) 599_616.

[4] Bhavna Makhija, VinitKumar Gupta and Indrajit Rajput, "Enhanced Data Security in Cloud Computing with Third Party Auditor", International Journal of Advanced Research in Computer Science and Software Engineering, Volume 3, Issue 2, February 2013 ISSN: 2277 128X.

[5] Abhishek Mohta,Ravi Kant Sahu and LK Awasthi, "Robust Data Security for Cloud while using Third Party Auditor" in International Journal of Advanced Research in Computer Science and Software Engineering, Vol No. 2, Issue 2,Feb 2012.

[6] Cong Wang and Kui Ren, Wenjing Lou and Jin Li, "Toward Publicly Auditable Secure Cloud Data Storage Services" ,IEEE Network July/August 2010

[7] Cong Wang, Qian Wang, Kui Ren, and Wenjing Lou, "Privacy-Preserving Public Auditing for Data Storage Security in Cloud Computing" , IEEE INFOCOM 2010, San Diego, CA, March 2010.

[8] A. Juels, J. Burton, and S. Kaliski, "PORs: Proofs of Retrievability for Large Files" , Proc. ACM CCS _07, Oct. 2007, pp. 584-97.

[9] Tauseef Ahmad, Mohammad Amanul Haque, Khaled Al-Nafjan and Asrar Ahmad Ansari, "Development of Cloud Computing and Security Issues", Information and Knowledge Management, Vol.3, No.1, 2013, ISSN 2224-5758.

[10] P. Trancoso and N. Angeli, "GridArchSim: Computer Architecture Simulation on the Grid", in Proc. CD of the 2nd European Across Grids Conference (AxGrids) 2004, 4 pages, January 2004.

[11] Daniel Nurmi, Rich Wolski, Chris Grzegorczyk, Graziano Obertelli, Sunil Soman, Lamia Youseff and Dmitrii Zagorodnov, "The eucalyptus open-source cloud-computing system", 9th IEEE/ACM International Symposium on Cluster Computing and the Grid, 2009. CCGRID '09.

[12] Won Kim: "Cloud Computing: Status and Prognosis", in Journal of Object Technology, vol. 8, no.1, January-February 2009, pp. 65-72

[13] Azza Abouzeid, Kamil Bajda-Pawlikowski, Daniel Abadi, Alexander Rasin and Avi Silberschatz, "HadoopDB: An Architectural Hybrid of MapReduce and DBMS Technologies for Analytical Workloads" ,In VLDB'09: Proceedings of the 2009 VLDB Endowment. Volume 2 Issue 1, August 2009, Pages 922-933.

[14] Amazon Web Service. Web Page: http://aws.amazon.com/ , Last date of access: 25th November, 2013

[15] Hadoop. Web Page: http://hadoop.apache.org , Last date of access: 25th November, 2013

[16] Windows Azure. Web Page: http://www.windowsazure.com/, Last date of access: 25th November, 2013

[17] Eucalyptus. Web Page: http://www.eucalyptus.com/, Last date of access: 25th November, 2013

[18] Openstack. Webpage: http://openstack.org/, Last date of access: 25th November, 2013

[19] Cloudsim. Webpage: http://www.cloudbus.org/cloudsim/, Last date of access: 25th November, 2013

[20] Console to Run and Maintain AWS. Webpage: https://console. aws.ama zon.c om/ ec2/v2/ home?region=ap-southeast-1#, Last date of access: 25th November, 2013

[21] Horton Hadoop Installetion guide. Web Page: https://sites.google.com/si te/howtohadoop/how-to-install-hdp#bm11, Last date of access: 25th November, 2013

[22] Election Commission Bangladesh: Web Site: http://www.ecs.gov.bd/En glish/, Last date of access: 25th November, 2013

[23] Voter Registration form: http://www.ecs.gov.bd/MenuExternalFilesEng/ 188.pdf, Last date of access: 25th November, 2013

[24] HadoopDB Guide. Web Page: http://hadoopdb.sourceforge.net/guide/, Last date of access: 25th November, 2013

[25] HadoopDB Guide. Web Page: http://www.coreservlets.com/hadoop-tutorial/, Last date of access: 25th November, 2013

[26] Sonali Yadav, "Comparative Study on Open Source Software for Cloud Computing Platform: Eucalyptus, Openstack and Opennebula", International Journal Of Engineering And Science, Vol.3, Issue 10, PP 51-54, October 2013, Issn:2319-6483.

[27] A. Pavlo, E. Paulson, A. Rasin, D. J. Abadi, D. J. DeWitt, S. Madden, and M. Stonebraker, "A Comparison of Approaches to Large-Scale Data Analysis", In SIGMOD, 2009.

[28] http://s3.amazonaws.com/public-repo-1.hortonworks.com/AMBARI-1.x/repos/centos6/AMBARI-1.x-1.el6.noarch.rpm 15th October, 2013.

[29] http://s3.amazonaws.com/public-repo-1.hortonworks.com/HDP-1.0.1.14/repos/centos6/hdp-release-1.0.1.14-1.el6.noarch.rpm 15th October, 2013.

[30] http://mirrors.ispros.com.bd/apache/hadoop/common/hadoop-1.1.2/   15th October, 2013.

[31] http://www.ubuntugeek.com/how-to-install-oracle-java-7-in-ubuntu-12-04.html 15th October, 2013.

[32] http://www.michael-noll.com/tutorials/running-hadoop-on-ubuntu-linux-single-node-cluster/ 15th October, 2013.

Appendix-I

Basic Information Entry form:

Code Information Entry GUI:

```
<!DOCTYPE html>
<html>
  <head>
    <meta http-equiv="Content-Type" content="text/html; charset=UTF-8">
    <title>Bangladesh People Search</title>
  </head>
  <body>
```

Basic Information Entry form

```html
<form action="Insert.php" method="post">
National ID: <input type="text" name="nid"><br>
Name in English: <input type="text" name="ename"><br>
Name: <input type="text" name="name"><br>
Father's Name: <input type="text" name="fname"><br>
Mother's Name: <input type="text" name="mname"><br>
Date of Birth (YY-MM-DD): <input type="text" name="dob"><br>
Gender::
<select name="gender">
<option value="M">M</option>
<option value="F">F</option>
<option value="U">U</option>
</select><br>
Religion:
<select name="religion">
<option value="Islam">Islam</option>
<option value="Hinduism">Hinduism</option>
<option value="Christianity">Christianity</option>
<option value="Buddhism">Buddhism</option>
<option value="Judaism">Judaism</option>
<option value="Other">Other</option>
</select><br>
Address: <input type="text" name="address"><br>
Blood Group:
<select name="bgroup">
<option value="A+">A+</option>
<option value="A-">A-</option>
<option value="B+">B+</option>
<option value="B-">B-</option>
<option value="AB+">AB+</option>
<option value="AB-">AB-</option>
<option value="O+">O+</option>
<option value="O_">O-</option>
</select><br>
Phone Number: <input type="text" name="phone"><br>
Qualification: <input type="text" name="qualification"><br>
```

Occupation: <input type="text" name="occupation">

<input type="submit">
</form>

    </body>
</html>

Verification GUI

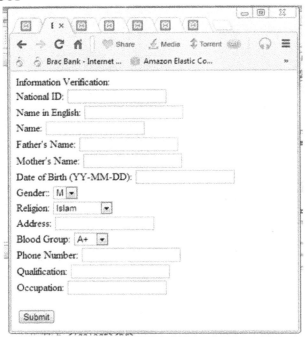

Verification GUI Code

```
<!DOCTYPE html>
<html>
   <head>
      <meta http-equiv="Content-Type" content="text/html; charset=UTF-8">
      <title>Bangladesh People Search</title>
   </head>
   <body>
```

Information Verification:
```
<form action="pull.php" method="post">
National ID: <input type="text" name="nid"><br>
Name in English: <input type="text" name="ename"><br>
Name: <input type="text" name="name"><br>
Father's Name: <input type="text" name="fname"><br>
Mother's Name: <input type="text" name="mname"><br>
Date of Birth (YY-MM-DD): <input type="text" name="dob"><br>
Gender::
<select name="gender">
<option value="M">M</option>
<option value="F">F</option>
<option value="U">U</option>
</select><br>
Religion:
<select name="religion">
<option value="Islam">Islam</option>
<option value="Hinduism">Hinduism</option>
<option value="Christianity">Christianity</option>
<option value="Buddhism">Buddhism</option>
<option value="Judaism">Judaism</option>
<option value="Other">Other</option>
</select><br>
Address: <input type="text" name="address"><br>
Blood Group:
<select name="bgroup">
<option value="A+">A+</option>
<option value="A-">A-</option>
<option value="B+">B+</option>
<option value="B-">B-</option>
<option value="AB+">AB+</option>
<option value="AB-">AB-</option>
<option value="O+">O+</option>
<option value="O_">O-</option>
</select><br>
Phone Number: <input type="text" name="phone"><br>
```

```
Qualification: <input type="text" name="qualification"><br>
Occupation: <input type="text" name="occupation"><br>
<br>
<input type="submit"><br>
</form>

  </body>
</html>
```

Pull SQL Instructions:

```
<?php

$con = mysqli_connect("localhost", "root", "", "bdps");
// Check connection
if (mysqli_connect_errno()) {
  echo "Failed to connect to MySQL: " . mysqli_connect_error();
}

$result = mysqli_query($con, "SELECT * FROM information WHERE
NID='$_POST[nid]'");
while ($row = mysqli_fetch_array($result)) {
  echo "For the National ID:";
  echo $row['NID'];
  echo "<br>";
  echo "<br>";
  echo "<br>";
  echo "Name:  ";
  echo $_REQUEST["ename"];
  if ($_REQUEST["ename"] == $row['E_name']) {
    echo ".......OK";
  } else {
    echo "XXXXXXXXXX...Wrong";
  }
  echo "<br>";
  echo "Name in Bangla:  ";
  echo $_REQUEST["name"];
```

```php
if ($_REQUEST["name"] == $row['Name']) {
    echo ".......OK";
} else {
    echo "XXXXXXXXXX...Wrong";
}

echo "<br>";
echo "Father's Name:  ";
echo $_REQUEST["fname"];
if ($_REQUEST["fname"] == $row['F_name']) {
    echo ".......OK";
} else {
    echo "XXXXXXXXXX...Wrong";
}
echo "<br>";
echo "Mother's Name:  ";
echo $_REQUEST["mname"];
if ($_REQUEST["mname"] == $row['M_name']) {
    echo ".......OK";
} else {
    echo "XXXXXXXXXX...Wrong";
}
echo "<br>";
echo "Date of Birth:  ";
echo $_REQUEST["dob"];
if ($_REQUEST["dob"] == $row['DOB']) {
    echo ".......OK";
} else {
    echo "XXXXXXXXXX...Wrong";
}
echo "<br>";
echo "Gender:  ";
echo $_REQUEST["gender"];
if ($_REQUEST["gender"] == $row['Gender']) {
    echo ".......OK";
```

```php
} else {
   echo "XXXXXXXXXX...Wrong";
}
echo "<br>";
echo "Religion:  ";
echo $_REQUEST["religion"];
if ($_REQUEST["religion"] == $row['Religion']) {
   echo ".......OK";
} else {
   echo "XXXXXXXXXX...Wrong";
}
echo "<br>";
echo "Address:  ";
echo $_REQUEST["address"];
if ($_REQUEST["address"] == $row['Address']) {
   echo ".......OK";
} else {
   echo "XXXXXXXXXX...Wrong";
}
echo "<br>";
echo "Blood Group:  ";
echo $_REQUEST["bgroup"];
if ($_REQUEST["bgroup"] == $row['B_group']) {
   echo ".......OK";
} else {
   echo "XXXXXXXXXX...Wrong";
}
echo "<br>";
echo "Phone Number:  ";
echo $_REQUEST["phone"];
if ($_REQUEST["phone"] == $row['Phone']) {
   echo ".......OK";
} else {
   echo "XXXXXXXXXX...Wrong";
}
echo "<br>";
```

```php
echo "Educational Qualification:  ";
echo $_REQUEST["qualification"];
if ($_REQUEST["qualification"] == $row['Qualification']) {
   echo ".......OK";
} else {
   echo "XXXXXXXXXX...Wrong";
}
echo "<br>";
echo "Occupation:  ";
echo $_REQUEST["occupation"];
if ($_REQUEST["occupation"] == $row['Occupation']) {
   echo ".......OK";
} else {
   echo "XXXXXXXXXX...Wrong";
}
echo "<br>";

}

mysqli_close($con);
?>
```

Bank Information Entry form:

Code for Bank Entry GUI:

```
<!DOCTYPE html>
<html>
  <head>
    <meta http-equiv="Content-Type" content="text/html; charset=UTF-8">
    <title>Bangladesh People Search</title>
  </head>
  <body>

Bank Entry Form
<form action="Insert_Bank.php" method="post">
National ID: <input type="text" name="nid"><br>
Bank Name: <input type="text" name="bname"><br>
Branch Name: <input type="text" name="brname"><br>
Account Number: <input type="text" name="accno"><br>
Card Number: <input type="text" name="cno"><br>
Type: <input type="text" name="acctype"><br>
<br>
<input type="submit"><br>
</form>
  </body>
</html>
```

SQL and Code for Bank record Insertion:
```php
<?php
$dt=date("Y-m-d");
$con=mysqli_connect("localhost","root","","bdps");
// Check connection
if (mysqli_connect_errno())
  {
  echo "Failed to connect to MySQL: " . mysqli_connect_error();
  }
$result = mysqli_query($con,"SELECT * FROM information WHERE NID='$_POST[nid]'");

while($row = mysqli_fetch_array($result))
  {
```

```
$NNID= $row['NID'];

$sql="INSERT INTO bank_acc_loan (BID, NID, Bank, Branch, Acc_no, Card_no,
Type, Date)
   VALUES
   (NULL,  '$NNID',    '$_POST[bname]',  '$_POST[brname]',  '$_POST[accno]',
'$_POST[cno]','$_POST[acctype]','$dt' )";
}

if (!mysqli_query($con,$sql))
{
die('Error: ' . mysqli_error($con));
}
echo "1 record added";

mysqli_close($con);
```

Bank Information Entry form:

Code for Bank record verification GUI:
```
<!DOCTYPE html>
<html>
   <head>
```

```
<meta http-equiv="Content-Type" content="text/html; charset=UTF-8">
<title>Bangladesh People Search</title>
</head>
<body>
```

Bank record verification Form
```
<form action="Bank_pull.php" method="post">
National ID: <input type="text" name="nid"><br>
Bank Name: <input type="text" name="bname"><br>
Branch Name: <input type="text" name="brname"><br>
Account Number: <input type="text" name="accno"><br>
Card Number: <input type="text" name="cno"><br>
Type: <input type="text" name="acctype"><br>
<br>
<input type="submit"><br>
</form>

</body>
</html>
```

Education Record Entry form:

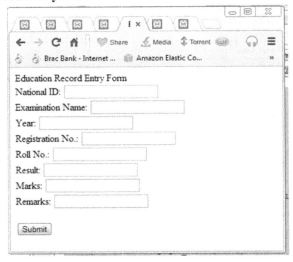

Code for Education Record Entry GUI:

```html
<!DOCTYPE html>
<html>
  <head>
    <meta http-equiv="Content-Type" content="text/html; charset=UTF-8">
    <title>Bangladesh People Search</title>
  </head>
  <body>

Education Record Entry Form
<form action="Insert_education.php" method="post">
National ID: <input type="text" name="nid"><br>
Examination Name: <input type="text" name="exname"><br>
Year: <input type="text" name="year"><br>
Registration No.: <input type="text" name="regno"><br>
Roll No.: <input type="text" name="rollno"><br>
Result: <input type="text" name="result"><br>
Marks: <input type="text" name="marks"><br>
Remarks: <input type="text" name="remarks"><br>
<br>
<input type="submit"><br>
</form>

  </body>
</html>
```

SQL and Code for Education record Insertion:

```php
<?php
$dt=date("Y-m-d");
$con=mysqli_connect("localhost","root","","bdps");
// Check connection
if (mysqli_connect_errno())
  {
  echo "Failed to connect to MySQL: " . mysqli_connect_error();
  }
```

```php
$result = mysqli_query($con,"SELECT * FROM information WHERE
NID='$_POST[nid]'");

while($row = mysqli_fetch_array($result))
  {
   $NNID= $row['NID'];

  $sql="INSERT INTO education (EID, NID, E_name, Year, Reg_no, Roll_no,
Result, Marks, Remarks)
   VALUES
   (NULL, '$NNID', '$_POST[exname]', '$_POST[year]', '$_POST[regno]',
'$_POST[rollno]','$_POST[result]','$_POST[marks]','$_POST[remarks]' )";



  }

if (!mysqli_query($con,$sql))
  {
  die('Error: ' . mysqli_error($con));
  }
echo "1 record added";
$exam=$_REQUEST["exname"];

$sql1="UPDATE information SET Qualification='$exam'
WHERE NID='$NNID'";

if (!mysqli_query($con,$sql1))
  {
  die('Error: ' . mysqli_error($con));
  }

mysqli_close($con);
```

Criminal Record Entry form:

Code for Criminal Record Entry GUI:

```
<!DOCTYPE html>
<html>
  <head>
    <meta http-equiv="Content-Type" content="text/html; charset=UTF-8">
    <title>Bangladesh People Search</title>
  </head>
  <body>

Criminal Record Entry Form
<form action="Insert_crime.php" method="post">
National ID: <input type="text" name="nid"><br>
File No.: <input type="text" name="recno"><br>
Case No.: <input type="text" name="caseno"><br>
Type: <input type="text" name="type"><br>
Place: <input type="text" name="place"><br>
Police Station: <input type="text" name="ps"><br>
Date: <input type="text" name="dt"><br>
Status: <input type="text" name="status"><br>
Details: <input type="text" name="details"><br>
<br>
<input type="submit"><br>
</form>
```

```
    </body>
</html>
```

SQL and Code for Criminal record Insertion:

```php
<?php
$dt=date("Y-m-d");
$con=mysqli_connect("localhost","root","","bdps");
// Check connection
if (mysqli_connect_errno())
  {
  echo "Failed to connect to MySQL: " . mysqli_connect_error();
  }
$result = mysqli_query($con,"SELECT * FROM information WHERE
NID='$_POST[nid]'");

while($row = mysqli_fetch_array($result))
  {
  $NNID= $row['NID'];

  $sql="INSERT INTO c_record (CID, NID, Rec_no, Case_no, Type, Place, PS,
Date, Status,Details)
    VALUES
    (NULL, '$NNID', '$_POST[recno]', '$_POST[caseno]', '$_POST[type]',
'$_POST[place]','$_POST[ps]','$_POST[dt]','$_POST[status]','$_POST[details]' )";

  }
if (!mysqli_query($con,$sql))
  {
  die('Error: ' . mysqli_error($con));
  }
echo "1 record added";

mysqli_close($con);
```

Job Record Entry form:

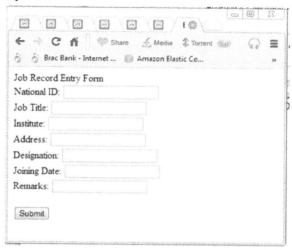

Code for Job Record Entry GUI:

```html
<!DOCTYPE html>
<html>
  <head>
    <meta http-equiv="Content-Type" content="text/html; charset=UTF-8">
    <title>Bangladesh People Search</title>
  </head>
  <body>

Job Record Entry Form
<form action="Insert_job.php" method="post">
National ID: <input type="text" name="nid"><br>
Job Title: <input type="text" name="title"><br>
Institute: <input type="text" name="institute"><br>
Address: <input type="text" name="address"><br>
Designation: <input type="text" name="designation"><br>
Joining Date: <input type="text" name="jdate"><br>
Remarks: <input type="text" name="remarks"><br>
<br>
```

```
<input type="submit"><br>
</form>

    </body>
</html>


SQL and Code for Job record Insertion:
<?php
$dt=date("Y-m-d");
$con=mysqli_connect("localhost","root","","bdps");
// Check connection
if (mysqli_connect_errno())
  {
  echo "Failed to connect to MySQL: " . mysqli_connect_error();
  }
$result = mysqli_query($con,"SELECT * FROM information WHERE
NID='$_POST[nid]'");

while($row = mysqli_fetch_array($result))
  {
   $NNID= $row['NID'];

  $sql="INSERT INTO job_record (JID, NID, Title, Institute, Address, Designation,
J_date, Remarks)
    VALUES
    (NULL, '$NNID', '$_POST[title]', '$_POST[institute]', '$_POST[address]',
'$_POST[designation]','$_POST[jdate]','$_POST[remarks]' )";


  }

if (!mysqli_query($con,$sql))
  {
  die('Error: ' . mysqli_error($con));
  }
```

```php
echo "1 record added";
$ttl=$_REQUEST["title"];

$sql1="UPDATE information SET Occupation='$ttl'
WHERE NID='$NNID'";

if (!mysqli_query($con,$sql1))
  {
  die('Error: ' . mysqli_error($con));
  }

mysqli_close($con);
```

Appendix-II

Appendix-II: Screen Shot of HiveQLs

```
ec2-54-254-211-125.ap-southeast-1.compute.amazonaws.com - PuTTY

2013-12-31 14:10:44,799 Stage-1 map = 100%,  reduce = 100%, Cumulative CPU 3.05 sec
MapReduce Total cumulative CPU time: 3 seconds 50 msec
Ended Job = job_201312231532_0027
Counters:
MapReduce Jobs Launched:
Job 0: Map: 1   Cumulative CPU: 3.05 sec   HDFS Read: 266 HDFS Write: 15 SUCCESS
Total MapReduce CPU Time Spent: 3 seconds 50 msec
OK
1        Narzu    Banini
Time taken: 45.776 seconds, Fetched: 1 row(s)
hive> select * from ty where (name="Narzu");
Total MapReduce jobs = 1
Launching Job 1 out of 1
Number of reduce tasks is set to 0 since there's no reduce operator
Starting Job = job_201312231532_0028, Tracking URL = http://ip-172-31-0-13.ap-southeast-1
jsp?jobid=job_201312231532_0028
Kill Command = /home/hadoop/bin/hadoop job  -kill job_201312231532_0028
Hadoop job information for Stage-1: number of mappers: 1; number of reducers: 0
2013-12-31 14:11:20,115 Stage-1 map = 0%,  reduce = 0%
2013-12-31 14:11:33,222 Stage-1 map = 100%,  reduce = 0%, Cumulative CPU 2.96 sec
2013-12-31 14:11:34,249 Stage-1 map = 100%,  reduce = 0%, Cumulative CPU 2.96 sec
2013-12-31 14:11:35,260 Stage-1 map = 100%,  reduce = 0%, Cumulative CPU 2.96 sec
2013-12-31 14:11:36,272 Stage-1 map = 100%,  reduce = 0%, Cumulative CPU 2.96 sec
2013-12-31 14:11:37,285 Stage-1 map = 100%,  reduce = 0%, Cumulative CPU 2.96 sec
2013-12-31 14:11:38,298 Stage-1 map = 100%,  reduce = 0%, Cumulative CPU 2.96 sec
2013-12-31 14:11:39,310 Stage-1 map = 100%,  reduce = 100%, Cumulative CPU 2.96 sec
MapReduce Total cumulative CPU time: 2 seconds 960 msec
Ended Job = job_201312231532_0028
Counters:
MapReduce Jobs Launched:
Job 0: Map: 1   Cumulative CPU: 2.96 sec   HDFS Read: 266 HDFS Write: 15 SUCCESS
Total MapReduce CPU Time Spent: 2 seconds 960 msec
OK
1        Narzu    Banini
Time taken: 42.694 seconds, Fetched: 1 row(s)
hive>
```

```
ec2-54-254-211-125.ap-southeast-1.compute.amazonaws.com - PuTTY

hive> ;
hive> ;
hive> drop table dict;
OK
Time taken: 1.946 seconds
hive> create table dict(word string) row format delimited fields terminated by ' ';
OK
Time taken: 0.141 seconds
hive> ;
hive> ;
hive>  load data local inpath 'dic.txt' into table dict;
Copying data from file:/home/hadoop/dic.txt
Loading data to table default.dict
Table default.dict stats: [num_partitions: 0, num_files: 1, num_rows: 0, total_size: 32
06080, raw_data_size: 0]
OK
Time taken: 8.681 seconds
hive>  load data local inpath 'dic.txt' into table dict;
Copying data from file:/home/hadoop/dic.txt
Loading data to table default.dict
Table default.dict stats: [num_partitions: 0, num_files: 2, num_rows: 0, total_size: 6412160,
 raw_data_size: 0]
OK
Time taken: 1.13 seconds
hive> drop table dict;
OK
Time taken: 0.415 seconds
hive> create table dict(word string) row format delimited fields terminated by ' ';
OK
Time taken: 0.1 seconds
hive>  load data local inpath 'dic.txt' into table dict;
Copying data from file:/home/hadoop/dic.txt
Loading data to table default.dict
Table default.dict stats: [num_partitions: 0, num_files: 1, num_rows: 0, total_size: 3206080,
 raw_data_size: 0]
OK
Time taken: 0.866 seconds
hive>
```

112

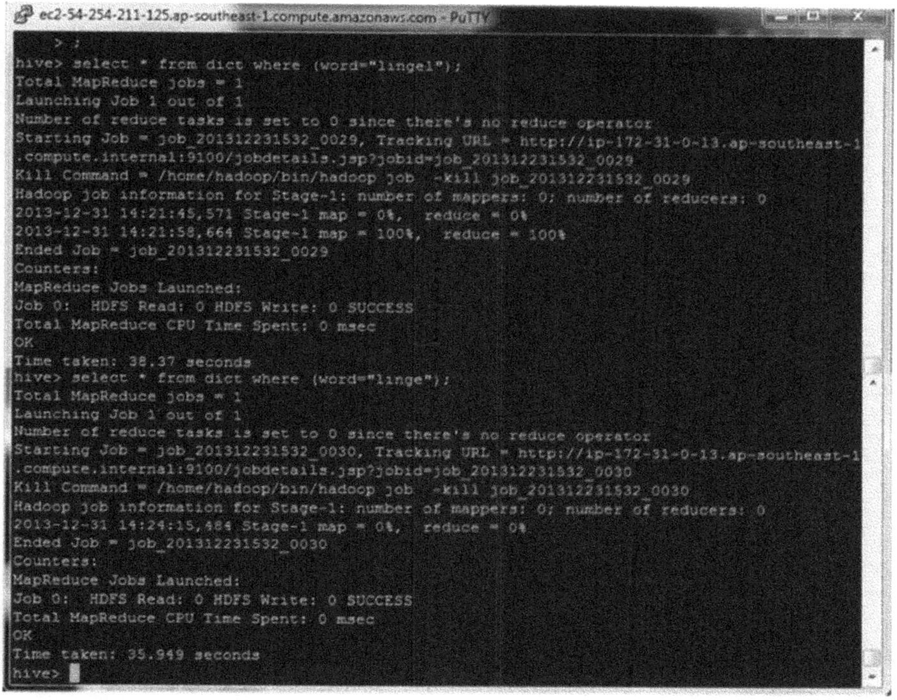
ec2-54-254-211-125.ap-southeast-1.compute.amazonaws.com - PuTTY
> ;
hive> select * from dict where (word="lingel");
Total MapReduce jobs = 1
Launching Job 1 out of 1
Number of reduce tasks is set to 0 since there's no reduce operator
Starting Job = job_201312231532_0029, Tracking URL = http://ip-172-31-0-13.ap-southeast-1
.compute.internal:9100/jobdetails.jsp?jobid=job_201312231532_0029
Kill Command = /home/hadoop/bin/hadoop job -kill job_201312231532_0029
Hadoop job information for Stage-1: number of mappers: 0; number of reducers: 0
2013-12-31 14:21:45,571 Stage-1 map = 0%, reduce = 0%
2013-12-31 14:21:58,664 Stage-1 map = 100%, reduce = 100%
Ended Job = job_201312231532_0029
Counters:
MapReduce Jobs Launched:
Job 0: HDFS Read: 0 HDFS Write: 0 SUCCESS
Total MapReduce CPU Time Spent: 0 msec
OK
Time taken: 38.37 seconds
hive> select * from dict where (word="linge");
Total MapReduce jobs = 1
Launching Job 1 out of 1
Number of reduce tasks is set to 0 since there's no reduce operator
Starting Job = job_201312231532_0030, Tracking URL = http://ip-172-31-0-13.ap-southeast-1
.compute.internal:9100/jobdetails.jsp?jobid=job_201312231532_0030
Kill Command = /home/hadoop/bin/hadoop job -kill job_201312231532_0030
Hadoop job information for Stage-1: number of mappers: 0; number of reducers: 0
2013-12-31 14:24:15,484 Stage-1 map = 0%, reduce = 0%
Ended Job = job_201312231532_0030
Counters:
MapReduce Jobs Launched:
Job 0: HDFS Read: 0 HDFS Write: 0 SUCCESS
Total MapReduce CPU Time Spent: 0 msec
OK
Time taken: 35.949 seconds
hive>

```
ec2-54-254-211-125.ap-southeast-1.compute.amazonaws.com - PuTTY

2013-12-31 14:43:32,028 Stage-1 map = 100%,  reduce = 0%, Cumulative CPU 5.12 sec
2013-12-31 14:43:33,039 Stage-1 map = 100%,  reduce = 0%, Cumulative CPU 5.12 sec
2013-12-31 14:43:34,050 Stage-1 map = 100%,  reduce = 0%, Cumulative CPU 5.12 sec
2013-12-31 14:43:35,060 Stage-1 map = 100%,  reduce = 0%, Cumulative CPU 5.12 sec
2013-12-31 14:43:36,070 Stage-1 map = 100%,  reduce = 0%, Cumulative CPU 5.12 sec
2013-12-31 14:43:37,081 Stage-1 map = 100%,  reduce = 0%, Cumulative CPU 5.12 sec
2013-12-31 14:43:38,091 Stage-1 map = 100%,  reduce = 100%, Cumulative CPU 5.12 sec
MapReduce Total cumulative CPU time: 5 seconds 120 msec
Ended Job = job_201312231532_0037
Counters:
MapReduce Jobs Launched:
Job 0: Map: 1   Cumulative CPU: 5.12 sec   HDFS Read: 3206294 HDFS Write: 5 SUCCESS
Total MapReduce CPU Time Spent: 5 seconds 120 msec
OK
bird
Time taken: 43.616 seconds, Fetched: 1 row(s)
hive> select * from dict where (word="bird");
Total MapReduce jobs = 1
Launching Job 1 out of 1
Number of reduce tasks is set to 0 since there's no reduce operator
Starting Job = job_201312231532_0038, Tracking URL = http://ip-172-31-0-13.ap-south
east-1.compute.internal:9100/jobdetails.jsp?jobid=job_201312231532_0038
Kill Command = /home/hadoop/bin/hadoop job  -kill job_201312231532_0038
Hadoop job information for Stage-1: number of mappers: 1; number of reducers: 0
2013-12-31 14:44:05,745 Stage-1 map = 0%,  reduce = 0%
2013-12-31 14:44:22,912 Stage-1 map = 100%,  reduce = 0%, Cumulative CPU 4.71 sec
2013-12-31 14:44:23,922 Stage-1 map = 100%,  reduce = 0%, Cumulative CPU 4.71 sec
2013-12-31 14:44:24,933 Stage-1 map = 100%,  reduce = 0%, Cumulative CPU 4.71 sec
2013-12-31 14:44:25,944 Stage-1 map = 100%,  reduce = 0%, Cumulative CPU 4.71 sec
2013-12-31 14:44:26,954 Stage-1 map = 100%,  reduce = 0%, Cumulative CPU 4.71 sec
2013-12-31 14:44:27,967 Stage-1 map = 100%,  reduce = 0%, Cumulative CPU 4.71 sec
2013-12-31 14:44:28,977 Stage-1 map = 100%,  reduce = 100%, Cumulative CPU 4.71 sec
MapReduce Total cumulative CPU time: 4 seconds 710 msec
Ended Job = job_201312231532_0038
Counters:
MapReduce Jobs Launched:
Job 0: Map: 1   Cumulative CPU: 4.71 sec   HDFS Read: 3206294 HDFS Write: 5 SUCCESS
Total MapReduce CPU Time Spent: 4 seconds 710 msec
OK
bird
Time taken: 45.954 seconds, Fetched: 1 row(s)
hive>
```

```
ec2-54-254-211-125.ap-southeast-1.compute.amazonaws.com - PuTTY

Hadoop job information for Stage-1: number of mappers: 1; number of reducers: 0
2013-12-31 14:40:54,151 Stage-1 map = 0%,  reduce = 0%
2013-12-31 14:41:07,283 Stage-1 map = 100%,  reduce = 0%, Cumulative CPU 4.69 sec
2013-12-31 14:41:08,294 Stage-1 map = 100%,  reduce = 0%, Cumulative CPU 4.69 sec
2013-12-31 14:41:09,306 Stage-1 map = 100%,  reduce = 0%, Cumulative CPU 4.69 sec
2013-12-31 14:41:10,317 Stage-1 map = 100%,  reduce = 0%, Cumulative CPU 4.69 sec
2013-12-31 14:41:11,327 Stage-1 map = 100%,  reduce = 0%, Cumulative CPU 4.69 sec
2013-12-31 14:41:12,338 Stage-1 map = 100%,  reduce = 0%, Cumulative CPU 4.69 sec
2013-12-31 14:41:13,352 Stage-1 map = 100%,  reduce = 100%, Cumulative CPU 4.69 sec
MapReduce Total cumulative CPU time: 4 seconds 690 msec
Ended Job = job_201312231532_0035
Counters:
MapReduce Jobs Launched:
Job 0: Map: 1   Cumulative CPU: 4.69 sec   HDFS Read: 3206294 HDFS Write: 0 SUCCESS
Total MapReduce CPU Time Spent: 4 seconds 690 msec
OK
Time taken: 42.367 seconds
hive> select * from dict where (word="brd");
Total MapReduce jobs = 1
Launching Job 1 out of 1
Number of reduce tasks is set to 0 since there's no reduce operator
Starting Job = job_201312231532_0036, Tracking URL = http://ip-172-31-0-13.ap-south
east-1.compute.internal:9100/jobdetails.jsp?jobid=job_201312231532_0036
Kill Command = /home/hadoop/bin/hadoop job  -kill job_201312231532_0036
Hadoop job information for Stage-1: number of mappers: 1; number of reducers: 0
2013-12-31 14:42:06,420 Stage-1 map = 0%,  reduce = 0%
2013-12-31 14:42:22,585 Stage-1 map = 100%,  reduce = 0%, Cumulative CPU 4.96 sec
2013-12-31 14:42:23,597 Stage-1 map = 100%,  reduce = 0%, Cumulative CPU 4.96 sec
2013-12-31 14:42:24,608 Stage-1 map = 100%,  reduce = 0%, Cumulative CPU 4.96 sec
2013-12-31 14:42:25,619 Stage-1 map = 100%,  reduce = 0%, Cumulative CPU 4.96 sec
2013-12-31 14:42:26,631 Stage-1 map = 100%,  reduce = 0%, Cumulative CPU 4.96 sec
2013-12-31 14:42:27,642 Stage-1 map = 100%,  reduce = 0%, Cumulative CPU 4.96 sec
2013-12-31 14:42:28,655 Stage-1 map = 100%,  reduce = 100%, Cumulative CPU 4.96 sec
MapReduce Total cumulative CPU time: 4 seconds 960 msec
Ended Job = job_201312231532_0036
Counters:
MapReduce Jobs Launched:
Job 0: Map: 1   Cumulative CPU: 4.96 sec   HDFS Read: 3206294 HDFS Write: 0 SUCCESS
Total MapReduce CPU Time Spent: 4 seconds 960 msec
OK
Time taken: 45.3 seconds
hive>
```

Appendix-III

Appendix-III: Netbeans

The JDK is a development environment for building applications, applets, and components using the Java programming language. The JDK includes tools useful for developing and testing programs written in the Java programming language and running on the Java platform.

Step-1

Open Netbeans (any version greater then 5.0) ,Go to file–>>new project

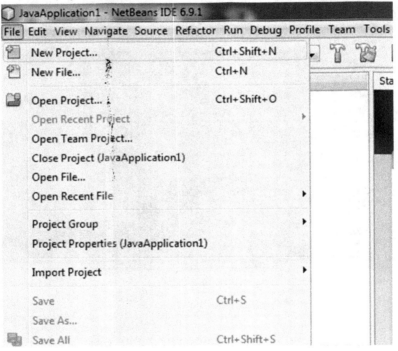

Step-2

select "Java" folder then select first option java Application ,Press next

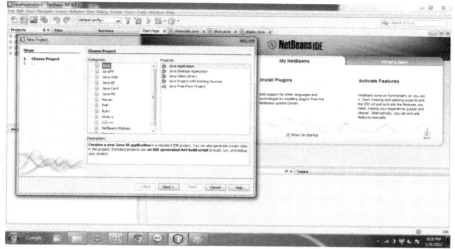

Step-3:

Now give name to the project as you wish , un-check the "create main class" press next.

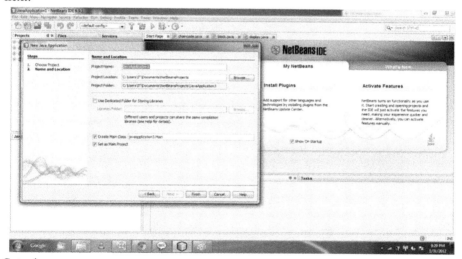

Setp-4

Now your project has been created as shown.

117

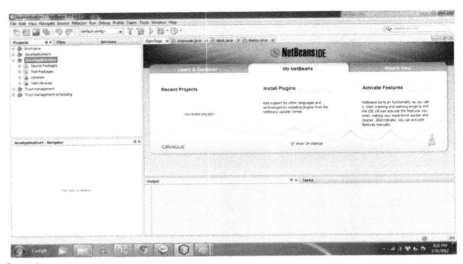

Step-5:

Go to library, right click on it, a menu will come, click on "Add jars/Folders"

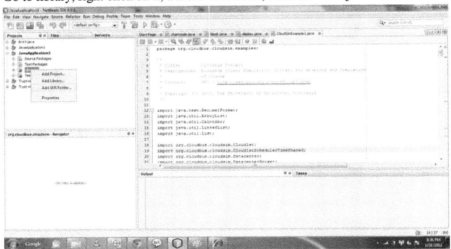

Step-6:

Now browse the cloudsim folder which you have extracted from zip file .and go to"cloudsim-2.1.1\jars" and select "cloudsim-2.1.1.jar".

Step-7

Now simply copy the "org" folder in "cloudsim-2.1.1\examples" and paste it to net beans source folder as shown.go to source and right click select paste.

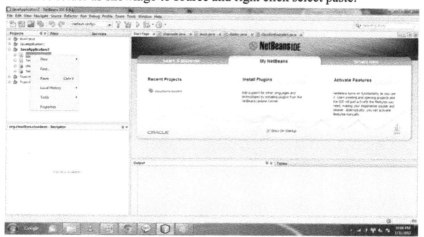

Step-8:

To run the example go to source ->> org.cloudbus.cloudsim.examples->>select any example ,right click on it and select "run" option the output will be displayed in the output window at the bottom.

119

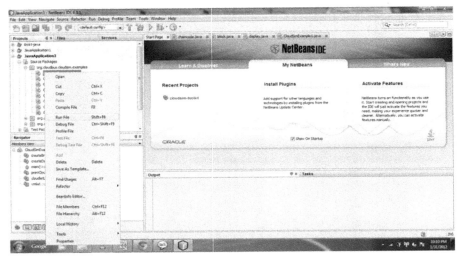

Output:

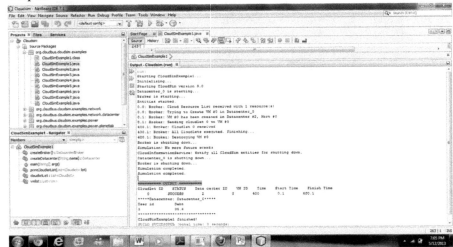

120